Secret Nature of

The
Isles of
Scilly

Secret Nature of

The
Isles of
Scilly

Andrew Cooper

Andrew Cooper

GREEN BOOKS

First published in 2006
by Green Books Ltd
Foxhole, Dartington, Totnes,
Devon TQ9 6EB
www.greenbooks.co.uk
info@greenbooks.co.uk

Design by Rick Lawrence
samskara@onetel.com

Printed by Cambrian Printers, Aberystwyth, Wales
Text printed on 100% recycled paper

A catalogue record for this publication
is available from the British Library

ISBN 1 903998 51 4

Facing page: Wall pennywort

Contents

Map of Scilly	8
Acknowledgements	10
Preface	11
How to Use this Book	12
How to Watch Wildlife	13
Introduction	18
Setting the Scene	21
Wild Highlights	34

THE ISLANDS — 36

Inhabited islands

St Mary's	39
Tresco	51
St Martin's	61
St Agnes and Gugh	67
Bryher	73

Uninhabited islands

Samson	81
Annet	85
St Helen's	93
Tean	94
Round Island	95
Men-a-vaur	97
Eastern Isles	101
Norrad Rocks	103
Western Rocks	104

WHERE TO FIND WILDLIFE — 107

Farmland, Shelterbelts and hedgerows,
Fresh Water, Gardens, Heathland,
Saline Lagoons, Sand Dunes,
Sea Cliffs, Sea Shore

PLANTS AND ANIMALS

Plants	127
Trees and shrubs	141
Birds	149
Mammals	175
Reptiles and Amphibians	183
Insects	185
Fish and Shellfish	209

Further Information	216
Index	217

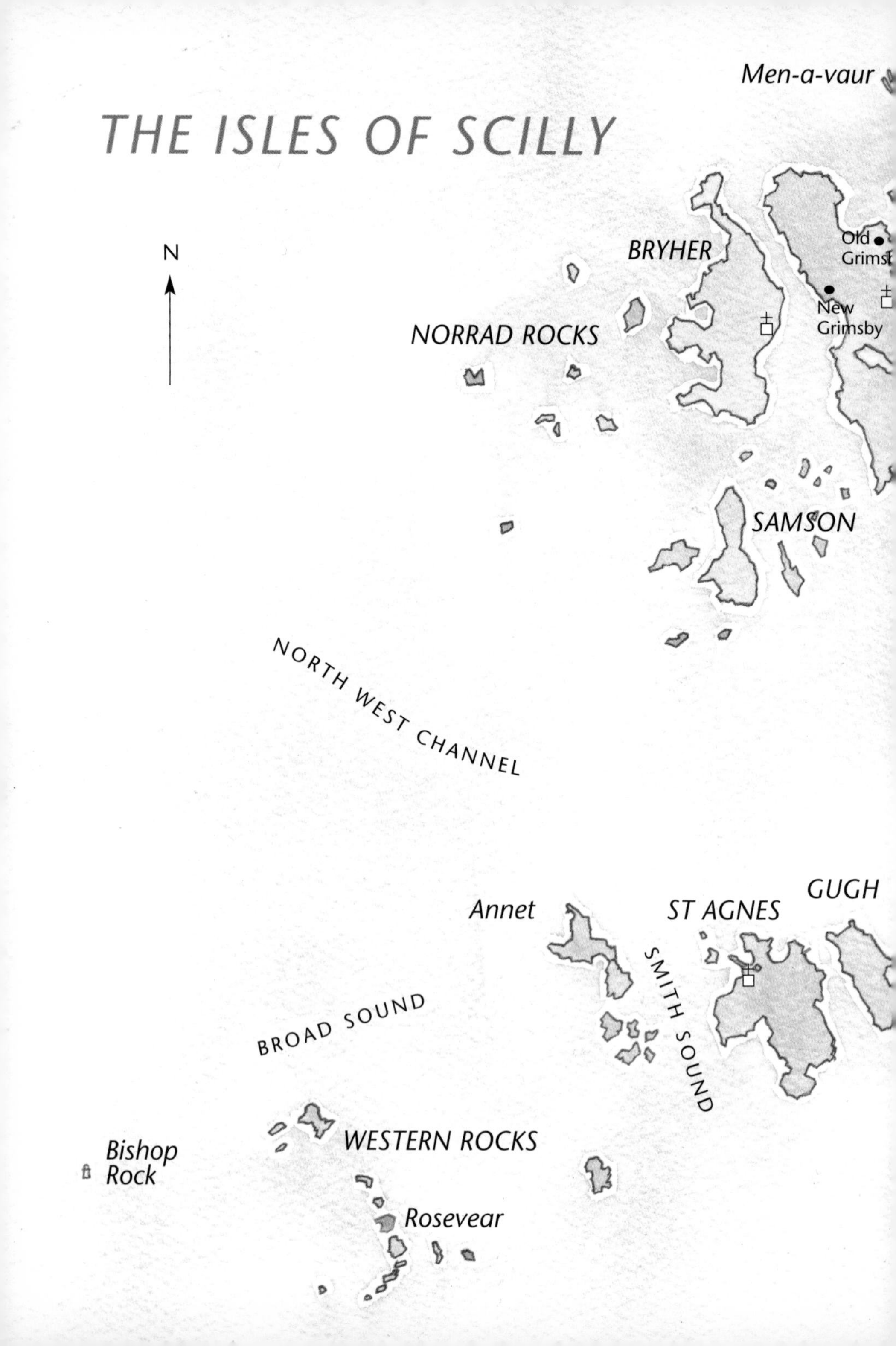

THE ISLES OF SCILLY

Men-a-vaur

N

BRYHER

Old
Grimsb

New
Grimsby

NORRAD ROCKS

SAMSON

NORTH WEST CHANNEL

Annet

ST AGNES

GUGH

BROAD SOUND

SMITH SOUND

Bishop
Rock

WESTERN ROCKS

Rosevear

Round
Island

White
Island

St Helen's

Tean

ST MARTIN'S

TRESCO

Crow Bar

EASTERN ISLES

THE ROAD

CROW SOUND

ST MARY'S

Hugh
Town

Airport

Old
Town

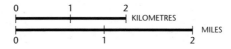

0	1	2	
			KILOMETRES

0	1	2
		MILES

Dedication

To the many wonderful days my family and I have spent in the islands and the many friends we have made over the years. The warmth of your welcome and wonderful sense of humour is always appreciated.

I would like to dedicate this book to my wife Jeanne for her encouragement and enthusiastic support as ever.

Acknowledgements

Many people have generously shared their knowledge and spared valuable time to help me celebrate the wonderful wildlife of Scilly in this book. I owe a great debt of thanks to all those who have so generously given their unstinting support and skills while filming in the islands and during this book's preparation. So many islanders – boatmen, farmers and landowners – have all welcomed and helped me in my quest, but especially the Rogers family from Lunnon, St Mary's, who have so patiently permitted me to explore and photograph their flower farm over the years. Also Mike Nelhams, Tresco Abbey Gardens, for his expert help and advice. I will always be indebted to Cyril Nicholas, boatman extraordinary, who not only landed me on so many small islands under difficult conditions but also got me off again.

I would particularly like to thank Jeremy Clitherow from English Nature, Truro office, for his invaluable assistance and specialist advice. Also the staff and volunteers of the Isles of Scilly Wildlife Trust, especially David Mawer for his advice on some of the uninhabited islands. Many others have also shared their specialist knowledge and enthusiasm. I would especially like to thank Professor James Scourse, marine geologist, for his remarkable insight into the island's past; Will Wagstaff and Nigel Hudson, Isles of Scilly Bird Group, for sharing their knowledge of the island's birdlife; Keith Hiscock, Marine Biological Association; Richard Warwick, Plymouth Marine Laboratories; Douglas Herdson, National Marine Aquarium; Steven Jones and David Smallshire, British Dragonfly Society; Rosemary Parslow, Botanical Society of the British Isles; and Michael Scott, Cornwall Moth Group.

Last but not least, my special thanks go to Green Books – John Elford, Amanda Cuthbert and team – for their considerable publishing talents and endless patience.

Preface

You have watched the wildlife programmes on television and read the books; now with the help of this guide you can come and meet some of the cast. Far more than just a simple guidebook, it is intended as a practical and inspirational companion to exploring the extraordinary wild richness of Scilly. It is part of a major new series of books covering the British Isles, compiled with help and advice from the island's own Wildlife Trust, the RSPB, Butterfly Conservation and many other organisations. The book title is from my most popular BBC natural history television series.

My aim is to make this book the next best thing to having your own personal guide as you explore the islands. You do not need to be an expert, just to have an appreciation of nature; it is intended as a companion for residents and visitors, adults and children in the beautiful Isles of Scilly. Profusely illustrated, it can be used on its own or with simple wildlife identification guides.

The British Isles support a greater diversity of wildlife and habitats than almost any other country of similar size in the world. The wildlife of Britain can be just as exciting and stimulating to watch as any big game in Africa, it is just more often than not on a smaller scale. There is another world outside people's everyday lives, a place where danger and death are common, and survival is only of the fittest. But you do not need to travel far to find one of the fastest predators on earth, see herds of grazing wild game or vast flocks of spectacular birds. They lie just beyond our doorstep, for this is the secret side of Britain – its nature.

Daffodils and lobster pot – flowers and fishing

How to Use this Book

After introducing you to the history and background of the Isles of Scilly, this book gives you an island-by-island guide to the best wildlife sites, walks and viewing points. For a quick reference to what makes Scilly special in terms of its nature, see the **Wild Highlights** box, and for a more detailed account turn to the **Plants and Wildlife** section. Here you will also find included the best month and time to look out for individual plants and animals. This section aims to introduce you to the extraordinary diversity of wildlife that can be found throughout the seasons, and includes brief descriptions of the different habitats to be found on the islands.

The next section, **How to Watch Wildlife**, gives you some of the tricks of the trade of a wildlife film maker. The information in this book has been compiled with the help and expertise of the principal wildlife conservation organisations involved in the islands, the Isles of Scilly Wildlife Trust, the RSPB and others. As Scilly is so wild, urban nature is not included separately. Most native plants and animals that can be found in gardens are also to be found in the surrounding countryside.

The calendar year has been split into seasons. While plants and most animals broadly keep to the same seasons as we do ourselves, birds are different.

Seasons for plants and most animals:

Spring	March – April	(Spring equinox: 21st March)
Summer	May – September	(Midsummer solstice: 21st June)
Autumn	October – November	(Autumn equinox: 21st September)
Winter	December – February	(Midwinter solstice: 21st December)

Bird seasons:

Spring	(migration)	March – May
Summer	(breeding)	June – July
Autumn	(migration)	August – November
Winter	(surviving)	December – February

While every effort has been made to ensure accuracy, the wildlife does not read the books we write about them. Nature is dynamic and forever changing. Also, every season new nature reserves open, paths and visitor facilities are being built or upgraded across the country. So why not help us to help you? Please let us know what you enjoyed most about this book. If your comments are included in future editions a complimentary copy will be sent to you. You can find our e-mail address and also keep up to date with the wildlife at the author's own farm in Devon by visiting www.wildlink.org.

How to Watch Wildlife

Scilly provides great opportunities to get close to wildlife. It is not that the creatures are tame, they are simply unafraid. It is an extraordinary privilege to get so close, even to common birds. The reason is probably that they are not routinely frightened by people. Indeed many of the migrant birds may never have seen a human before! The only way to watch wildlife in the islands is on foot – or even better by boat.

Watching any wild animal is a battle of wits – yours against a creature's natural instinct to survive. To enjoy wild behaviour – bird courtship displays or bull seals fighting – you do not need to get very close, but it is a particular thrill to watch a wild animal from just a few paces away. To get close you may need some of our now less-used senses. Instinct is a powerful ally. If you are not sure what to do just follow your natural feelings. Keeping still and quiet is the simplest way to enjoy successful wildlife watching, but real life is never quite like that. Many birds and insects are quite easy to approach if it is done slowly and with care. With the exception of owls,

Grey seal pup

most birds react more to movement than sound. Mammals are more difficult. Most of our mammals have amazingly keen senses of smell and hearing. Some also have acute eyesight and bats can 'see' you in pitch dark. Even insects have remarkably good sight – try getting close to a butterfly. It can be done if you approach very slowly, especially when the air temperature is cool in early morning. Just think and move like a chameleon!

At first, to increase your chances of success, try visiting places where wildlife is already accustomed to the presence of people – parks, gardens and nature reserves. Stay on the paths and wild creatures will often ignore you; step off a regular track and they will be gone.

Timing your visit is crucial. Not all plants and animals can be seen all year round but every season has its highlights. It is important to check the local tide times, both for your own safety and the best opportunity of seeing the most wildlife. The best time for watching many creatures is often early in the day but wind and weather also play their part. On a lake or pond in summer the leeward shore will have the most wind-blown insects, and that is where most birds and fish are likely to be feeding. But if a gale is blowing most birds seek shelter in the lee of reeds or banks.

Some creatures are also so rare that they are protected by law. Bats may not be disturbed at any time, many birds are fully protected, and others must not be approached at or near their nest. Check with English Nature or your County Wildlife Trust for a full, up-to-date list of all UK protected plants and animals.

When attempting to get close to a particular creature, beware other animals taking fright, alerting everything in the neighbourhood. Be aware too of your silhouette and shadow. Stay away from the skyline and keep a bush, tree or hillside behind you to disguise your human outline. It is often easier to get close to a creature on windy days than on calm, still days when sound carries far. Walk into or across the wind. In mist, many skulking birds such as warblers seem much bolder. Keep to softer ground, rather than walking on noisy stones. On dry crunchy vegetation, try waiting for a gust of wind to disguise the sound of footsteps.

Wearing neutral-coloured clothing, sturdy footwear and a good pair of binoculars all add to your chances of success. And knowing something about the behaviour of wild animals is also helpful. Some creatures are surprisingly curious. If you freeze for a few moments, they may come back for a second look at you. And if all else fails when you are wearing bright colours on a calm sunny day, and there is no way you can conceal yourself, just try pretending you are not remotely interested. Walk casually past without looking directly at the creature. Usually wild animals only stare at another creature for two reasons – a threat or a potential meal.

Wild flowers are far easier to approach – they cannot run away. But they can be more difficult to find. The biggest danger with plants is that you may accidentally trample them.

The best tip I can give for successful wildlife watching is to stop, look and listen more often. Just because you cannot see anything, it does not mean you cannot be seen. Good watching!

The Secret Nature Country Code

Enjoy the countryside and respect its life and work.

Guard against all risk of fire.

Leave gates as you find them; if in doubt close them.

Dogs should be kept under close control at all times.

Keep to public marked paths across farmland and marked trails on nature reserves.

Use gates and stiles to cross fences, hedges and walls.

Make no unnecessary noise – you will see and hear more wildlife.

Leave livestock, crops and machinery alone.

Take your litter home.

Help to keep all water clean.

Take special care on country roads – keep your speed down, especially near horses.

Cyclists should keep to bridleways, byways and special cycle routes.

Do not use motorised vehicles on footpaths and bridleways.

And in Scilly especially, resist the temptation to touch any wildlife!

Finally in the most remote areas I like the simple 'Take only pictures, leave only footprints', although personally I do not even like to leave footprints – they may spoil my next photograph!

Annet Head, with Thrift   *Overleaf: aerial picture of St Mary's*

Introduction

Sharks, palm trees and fine white sandy beaches with crystal clear seas – beneath a vivid blue sky these are the vital ingredients for any subtropical paradise. Add sunken treasure, corals and colourful, exotic flowers and you may well be forgiven for thinking you are a thousand miles from England. You would be mistaken.

The legendary lost land of Lyonesse was said to lie at the edge of the world, somewhere beyond Land's End. Ancient stories tell of a landscape drowned by rising seas. Yet just 28 miles off the extreme south-west tip of England the most isolated inhabited islands in Britain can still be found. The Isles of Scilly are among the most scenically beautiful islands in British waters. Separated from the mainland for thousands of years, surrounded by the vastness of the Atlantic Ocean, their remoteness is highlighted by the fact that they are one of the few places in Britain where the sun both rises and sets at sea all year round.

The Isles of Scilly claim to be England's only subtropical shores or islands. Here summer brings sparkling seas gently lapping the soft sand, while the sound of seabirds fills the fresh air and others of their kind sip nectar beneath the shade of towering palms. But there is another side to this paradise, a wild and exhilarating side open to the full fury of the Atlantic. Standing on the westernmost headland of Tresco is like travelling back in time because here the low-growing heather is part of a primeval landscape. Yet just half an hour's walk away you can enter another world. Any doubts about the island's subtropical claim are soon dispelled on entering the Abbey Gardens. Few places on earth can offer such startling contrasts in a single season as Scilly.

Since Stone Age people first ventured to the edge of their known world, the islands have been held in awe as a timeless, mystical place. Prehistoric tombs and ancient settlements still litter the land although some have been claimed by rising sea levels. Bathed in ocean currents generated

Sunken treasure: shells, china and a flint tool

from the tropical Gulf Stream, warm water creatures flourish in plankton-rich seas. Few places in Britain can boast a climate so mild – where frosts are rare and snow a remarkable event.

Scilly is without doubt a special place, distinct from the distant mainland. Lying at a crossroads in nature, the islands support a distinctive blend of common and exotic plants and animals. But this is also a wild land ruled by wind and tide, where large marine predators bask on the rocks and raucous colonies of strange nocturnal birds can fill the midnight air.

Today there are five inhabited islands – St Mary's, St Martin's, Tresco, Bryher and St Agnes – 40 smaller islands with vegetation, and some 150 named rocks. St Mary's is the biggest island by far, but even that is small. If one could walk straight across its widest point, from south to north it would take less than an hour. Even following the narrow roads, tracks and rutted lanes from the eroded smooth granite headland of Peninnis to the heights of Halangy Down does not take much longer. The islands' natural importance can be measured by the wealth of Sites of Special Scientific Interest – 26 so far. It is also a marine environment of great importance and officially designated an Area of Outstanding Natural Beauty, a Conservation Area, a Heritage Coast, a European Area of Special Conservation, and holds Ramsar status, which is only awarded to wetlands of international importance. Underwater, the lost lands flooded by seas in past millennia are now littered with the rusting remains of shipwrecks and richly colonised by sea life. In the deepest water, brilliant jewel anemones and cup corals carpet the rocks.

Following the swell into the shallows between the main islands at low tide can be a nerve-racking experience for all but the most experienced island boatmen. Among terrifying fingers of hard rock, the exposed fronds of vast undersea Kelp forests can be seen breaking the surface. In more sheltered parts, the Kelp gives way to marine meadows of Eel Grass. Cliffs and boulder-strewn coasts defend the outer edge of the islands, while fine sandy beaches topped with grassy dunes, ring the inner shores.

Prickly-fruited buttercup

| 19 |

Walking through the seasons in Scilly can bring a surprise around each corner and in every cove. While the mainland still shivers in the last throes of winter, spring arrives early in the islands with an explosion of blooms. Fields of Daffodil and Narcissus now open faster than they can be picked. The flower farmer's frantic winter season is drawing to a close. What follows is a colourful succession of cultivated and wild flowers throughout the summer months.

Spring also brings the first seasonal influx of migrants – birds and their watchers. The islands have an enviable reputation as one of the best birding places on earth. At times it is more like an international avian airport, with flights arriving and leaving throughout the day and night. Here strange little birds flit from hedge to hedge, and warblers, waders and wildfowl are all scrutinised by an army of telescope-toting enthusiasts.

Easter sees the arrival of the first holidaymakers and children playing in the sand. Seabirds start nesting on the off-islands and seals sunbathe on the rocks. As the season unfolds, Sea Pinks paint the coastline, gardens overflow with exotic hues and yellow gorse mixes with purple Heather spreading across the cliffs. On a fine day the view from the highest point on St Mary's is magnificent. Looking out over the calm blue waters of Crow Sound, the scattering of islands seems unreal for a part of England, more Caribbean than Cornwall, a white-beached archipelago set in a tropical blue sea. And the wildlife is no less extraordinary. From Puffins gathering on their favourite rocks to great fishing fleets of Shag in the tide, Scilly Bees and Continental Shrews, even living sticks with legs, and a remarkably rare ant, the island's nature never ceases to surprise.

Summer has hardly finished before the first crops of flowers begin to show again. Then the plaintive cries of seal pups mark the summer's end and the autumn equinox, heralding the first of the season's gales. But even the wind in Scilly brings wild bounty as the first migrant birds fly in. Thousands more may follow over the next few weeks. Separated from the mainland for so many millennia, Scilly has a truly remarkable natural history that sets these isles apart from the rest of Britain.

St Mary's harbour

Setting the Scene –
geology, first people and climate

The Isles of Scilly have a natural significance out of all proportion to their size. Their remoteness, a long and visible human history and an extreme maritime climate, has given them a status of international importance. Their importance to people in the past cannot be denied. No other place in the British Isles boasts so many prehistoric tombs in such a small area. Indeed the number is so great that Scilly was once considered a sacred isle, a burial place for kings. It was even claimed to be the destination of King Arthur's last voyage after his famous final battle, but the truth is far more exciting.

GEOLOGY

The British Isles consist of some 6,289 islands, of which some 200 make up the Isles of Scilly. They are mainly composed of some of the hardest volcanic rocks formed around 290 million years ago – granite. Today the granite roots of the once great Armorican mountain chain form the backbone to the entire south-west peninsula. At one time these mountains were colossal peaks. Time and tide eventually eroded most of their softer rocks away. Now only a massive undulating granite spine remains, stretching from Dartmoor in Devon, through Bodmin Moor in Cornwall and then way out into the Atlantic. Beyond Scilly lies Haig Fras, a great sunken granite outcrop over 60 miles from Land's End.

The granite itself has a distinctive crystalline and coarse-grained texture which can be seen in the many exposed rocks and the variety of attractively coloured, sea-smoothed pebbles. This granite produces the relatively poor, acidic soils of the islands.

The Isles of Scilly are the only archipelago in England. They are low-lying islands and even the largest, St Mary's, is barely 50 metres at its highest point. The archipelago itself is perched on a submarine shelf rising steeply from the sea floor. This relatively flat-topped granite plateau is scattered with summits forming either submerged reefs, protruding bare rocks or larger green islands. The water dividing them is surprisingly shallow, in places less than waist deep at the lowest tide. If sea levels were to drop just 10 metres, most of the main islands would be reunited. With a drop of 20 metres, even St Agnes, Annet and the Western Rocks would join the rest.

The entire archipelago is encircled by a sharp 50-metre-deep contour. In places this undersea cliff comes to within a few hundred metres of the northern, eastern and southern shores. As the prevailing winds and sea swell arrive from the south-west, and with deep water just offshore, the islands here are extremely exposed. These outer isles form a granite bastion protecting the most sheltered shores from the fury of Atlantic storms. This is also the first and last landfall for shipping entering one of the busiest seaways in the world, a mariner's nightmare of jagged reefs and hidden ledges guarding the north-west approach to the English Channel. The impressive Bishop Rock lighthouse, rising nearly 55 metres above high water, marks its treacherous far western end. The Western Rocks endure some of the most exposed sea conditions anywhere in western Europe and among the worst in the British Isles.

SEA AND ICE

The south-western landscape was shaped by two powerful forces in more recent millennia – sea and ice. During some points in their history the islands were probably completely submerged. Yet at other times, during the coldest periods, sea levels were much lower than at present and Scilly became part of the mainland. Then it would have been possible to walk from Spain to Ireland, across the vast low-lying plain that today forms the submerged continental shelf. The raised plateau that would eventually become the Isles of Scilly would no doubt have provided magnificent views over the great valley that now forms the English Channel.

The other major influence on the landscape was just as devastating as the sea. For thousands of years snow and ice periodically covered much of the British Isles.

Porthloo showing head deposits in distance

So far there have been four major ice ages, the last ending over 10,000 years ago. During the coldest times immense glaciers, some hundreds of metres thick, covered most of Britain except for the far south-west. Yet even here conditions were extreme, much like parts of Alaska today. Winter pack ice would have extended far offshore. At their greatest extent the glaciers just reached the northern edge of the plateau and rocky peaks that one day would become the Isles of Scilly.

Repeated freezing and thawing shattered exposed rock, and the resulting rubble and mud mix poured down every slope, smoothing sharp edges and covering cliffs. The thick ice sheets also eroded the rock over which they passed, eventually depositing sand, gravel and clays. Many layers were left over the granite rocks of Scilly. The fine sand left behind can still be seen today, forming brilliant white beaches and soft dunes. The so-called 'head' deposits of brown mud and stone are also clearly visible in the island's low cliffs. At Porthloo on St Mary's these head deposits are among the deepest in the islands, several metres thick.

Between the periods of intense cold, warmer, almost tropical, conditions at times prevailed. This caused the ice to melt and sea levels to rise even higher than they are today. Traces of wave-cut platforms in the cliffs and 'raised beaches' with sand and sea-washed stones 3-8 metres above present-day high water, can still be seen in places. Today evidence also suggests that while sea levels are rising again, the entire granite archipelago is also still slowly sinking – but the combined effect only adds up to just a few millimetres a year.

The ending of the last ice age must have presented a remarkable scene around 10,000 years ago. Sea levels were rising fast, summers getting warmer, starting earlier and lasting longer. Soon the island's link to the mainland was again severed by the sea, yet it was still many metres lower than at present. Then the panoramic view from the north-west heights of St Mary's, looking across to the peaks of the Eastern Isles and around to the island of Samson, would have been almost unrecognisable – a single large island largely covered by trees. Only the tallest hills, coastal cliffs and granite outcrops might have seemed familiar.

THE LOST LANDS OF SCILLY

Scilly poses a problem. It is a mystery of few facts, riddled with speculation. Trying to explain the presence of some of the islands' more interesting wild animals and plants is not easy. What is known is that over the last two million years, sea levels have changed dramatically, but precisely when and by how much is not so easy to tell. However, it could be the key to understanding the enigma of an alien ant and some of the island's more unusual plants.

Around 18,000 years ago the rocky plateau of Scilly towered above the surrounding freezing windswept land. In the depths of the last ice age sea levels were around 130 metres lower than at present. Although it was not as severe as previous ice ages and southern England remained largely free of ice sheet, the soil would still have been frozen. Plants struggle to survive in such conditions as Arctic tundra.

As global temperatures began to rise, so too did sea levels. It continued apace, apart from a couple of climate hiccups when the Gulf Stream appears rather alarmingly to have stopped flowing, first for just over a thousand years around 12,000 years ago, and again around 8,200 years ago for about three centuries. But across the planet temperatures still continued to rise.

Head deposits (soil and gravel deposits during an ice age)

Until recently Scilly was thought to have severed its last link with the mainland over 14,000 years ago. If so, there is a problem. How can the presence of some of the islands' so-called Lusitanian wildlife be explained? Today these special plants and animals are commonly found only much further south, in France and Spain. No proof of a later land bridge existed – until recently.

Now compelling new evidence suggests that a land bridge did remain until much more recent times. During the last ice age the glaciers only reached as far south as a line from London to Bristol. When the ice finally started melting, sea levels began to rise and a window of opportunity arose. Before the Atlantic Ocean returned to drown the great valleys forming the English Channel and Irish Sea, the land that was to become the British Isles basked in a rapidly warming climate, perhaps lasting for 2,000 years or more. New research suggests that sometime between 14,000 and 11,000 years ago the Spanish peninsula was linked by dry land through Brittany and Scilly, perhaps as far as Ireland. For a time the exposed continental shelf still formed a land bridge uniting the British Isles with the Continent and the climate was still warming fast. Free of snow and ice, with summers becoming warmer and winters not so severe, new wild travellers could arrive and survive.

Carried on the wind, some seeds and small flying insects can journey many miles. Others spread more slowly. At the end of the last cold period, as the ice retreated north and the climate continued to warm, more plants and animals spread up from the Mediterranean regions. Just imagine the scene at the northernmost limit of trees, standing among a straggling line of stunted conifers. Arctic tundra is a desolate-looking place at the best of times, where only low-growing plants stretch to the northern skyline. Permanently frozen ground prevents deep-rooted trees from growing. It is also a dangerous place. Great herds of Caribou attract packs of Wolves, and roaming Bears are hungry for a meal.

But when the world began to warm during the inter-glacial summer, and winter snow had retreated, a short walk out across the boggy tundra beyond the Arctic tree-line would yield a real surprise. Among the ground-hugging Heather and tiny stunted Arctic Willow, new life would be found. Way out beyond the existing tree-line, young pine trees would be germinating and growing well. This was global warming on a grand scale, the natural world on the move. Here trees marched with the help of the wind, as well as forgetful squirrels and absent-minded jays carrying seeds out to bury them beyond the edge of the existing forest. Over the centuries that followed in the wake of Pine and Birch, came great woodlands of Oak and Hazel, along with many other trees and their animal life, all slowly spreading north.

As the climate continued to warm, western Europe became a landscape largely covered by vast primeval forest, but sea levels continued to rise and drown low-lying areas. By 6,000 years ago the great valley dividing southern England from France was finally flooded. Britain had become an island once more and colonisation by land ceased. Creatures that could neither swim nor fly, and plants unable to spread far and wide by the wind, could no longer reach these islands. Those species that had already arrived in Scilly were now marooned.

There are few places in the British Isles where the impact of rising sea levels and sinking land can be so graphically seen as on the Isles of Scilly. It is an extraordinary thought that the first people to arrive here may have walked. During Arctic summers nomadic hunters roamed the shores of western Europe. By 8,000 years ago Oak and Hazel, with scattered stands of Ash and Elm, covered the landscape of Scilly. In the most exposed coastal areas, Birch scrub survived better. By the time the English Channel finally formed some 6,000 years ago, people could only have reached these islands by boat. Timber was used for building houses and boats, and as fuel for fires. By 2,500 years ago the decline in tree cover had produced a more open landscape of fields, pasture and heathland similar to today, but sea levels continued to rise.

When Roman ships moored off Scilly the shape of many of the islands' outer edges was beginning to take shape. Even at the time of the Norman Conquest, around 1,000 years ago, most of the islands apart from St Agnes were probably still joined at low water. It was not until Tudor ships began to anchor in Crow Sound that the present island outlines were finally formed. How do we know this? The best evidence comes from place names. Old Cornish names dating from the sixteenth century can be found around the outer edges of the islands, but later Tudor English names appear to be confined to the inner shores. So perhaps the final separation of St Mary's, St Martin's, Tresco, Bryher and Samson occurred little more than 500 years ago.

Just when and how the inundation happened we can only guess. But it is likely that destructive storm surges were to blame. Exceptionally high tides combined with extreme low-pressure weather conditions result in the large-scale drowning of low-lying areas of land. The effect on Scilly was dramatic. The power of waves and weight of water shifted large granite boulders, scoured out softer 'head' deposits and swept away entire dunes of sand.

Even more terrifying is the thought that the same result might have been caused by a tsunami. There is good evidence for two such events in the south-west of England and there may be more so far undetected. It is now thought that the terrible flood that drowned large parts of the Somerset Levels in 1709 was caused by a 10-metre-high wall of water surging far inland. In 1755 a tsunami produced by the devastating Lisbon earthquake off Portugal probably swept sand into pools on St Agnes and sent a 3-metre-high wave far up the Tamar valley in Devon. Whatever the cause, storm surge or tsunami, the consequences of massive inundation by the sea must have terrified the islanders of the day and contributed to the shaping of the archipelago we see today. Many early settlements, houses, fields and graves now lie submerged. At low tide, stone walls can still be found drowned in the shallows. Although probably of more ancient origin, it is possible that these walls were still in use during Roman times, and even by early Tudor farmers. On small islands where land is at a premium, the story of human habitation is inextricably linked with its natural history. Few places in Britain reveal so dramatically such a remarkable story of people and the power of nature.

ISLAND PEOPLE

The Mesolithic Period saw bands of semi-nomadic people, hunting and gathering food, moving with the seasons. Remarkably, some evidence survives to provide a tantalising glimpse of their lifestyle. Preserved pollen from peat deposits on St Mary's Higher Moors, suggests that early people may have used fire to flush out wild animals, clear scrub and improve grazing. Virgin forest seems to have given way to scattered Birch trees and lush pasture. When Scilly was a single large landmass, the presence of Oak woodland in the sheltered valleys could have supported herds of Red Deer, perhaps even Wild Boar and other game.

The Neolithic Period witnessed the dawning of agriculture. The domestication of animals and increasing cultivation of plants for food heralded a more settled way of life. Hunting and gathering still played an important part but more permanent settlements gave rise to a more sophisticated social community. Tribes marked their presence with the erection of large stone monuments, megaliths, for ritual or territorial purposes. Pollen analysis reveals another change around 5,000 years ago. Increasing clearance of the ancient wildwood and the cultivation of more cereal crops was followed by an apparent decline in farming and the return of woodland.

The Bronze Age saw the first permanent communities arrive in the islands from west Cornwall. Over eighty impressive entrance graves from this period have been discovered in Scilly. More mysterious rocks, often called megaliths, can still be seen on the islands. These people farmed and fished, hunted, gathered and scavenged food to make a living. A large variety of birds were hunted for their meat, feathers and oil. Many are obviously not as common as they once were. Apart from the sea birds, Razorbill, Guillemot and Gannet, they hunted Goose, Raven, White Stork and even the occasional Swan. Red Deer and Wild Horse, Pig, Dolphin and Seal probably provided a good roast meal. A stranded Whale would have been a rare but welcome prize, a valuable extra supply of oil for lighting, supplementing the more usual source from Seals.

View from Samson over Norrad Rocks

Early strains of barley and wheat were grown in fields of cereal crops, as well as beans and pulses. Dwarf breeds of sheep and ox, and a surprisingly small semi-wild pig with large feet roamed the land. Fishing was an important source of food all year and fish was also preserved by drying in the wind or salted. The catch included most of the species still found in the island waters, including Cod, Saithe, Sea Bream, Bass, Pollack, Ling, Gurnard, Gilthead, Wrasse, Conger, Turbot and Plaice. Huge quantities of limpet shells suggest substantial quantities may have been used as bait, as well as for food. Other shellfish included Cockles, Whelks and Topshells, along with Scallops, whose large shells were also used to hold lamp oil for lighting.

While it is feasible that creatures such as Roe and Red deer, as well as Pallas' Vole arrived much earlier when the land bridge was still present, their remains from Bronze Age settlements suggest that some may have been imported for food and skins. This is supported by the fact that other wild mammals, such as Fox, Badger, Weasel and Stoat never seemed to have reached Scilly. Other small creatures may simply have stowed away amongst food stores traded from the mainland of England, France or Spain.

The Iron Age arrived late in Scilly, with little major impact on the islanders' seemingly well established way of life. Increasing trade with the mainland eventually introduced change, but the greatest alteration to the islanders' way of life was in the construction of forts. Three cliff castles were constructed, on Bryher, St Mary's and St Martin's, but at that time they were situated about the same distance apart on the same large island.

Shag

The first written reference to the Isles of Scilly came with the Roman invasion of Britain. Mention was made of *Insula Sillina* by classical writers during the first few centuries of the Roman occupation of the mainland. However, the Empire's influence over the islands appears to have been minimal. By now all pigs seemed to be domesticated and Red Deer had vanished, while dogs and rabbits made their first appearance. A wider variety of fish now featured on the islanders' menu, including Common Eel, Mullet, Whiting and John Dory. The birdlife of Scilly also seemed to be increasing, giving a clear indication of a changing environment or perhaps a taste for different food. Pools of brackish water attracted wildfowl – Teal, Long-tailed Duck and Scaup, along with White Stork, Common Snipe, Bittern, Heron, Swan and perhaps Moorhen. More exciting is the evidence for Chough being found on the islands. Some remains of what may well be these birds were discovered on St Martin's dating from some time between the second and seventh centuries AD.

The people of Scilly also seem to have escaped the occasional Anglo-Saxon raids in Cornwall. Trade with the Mediterranean, France and Ireland, however, gave the islanders their first contact with Christianity. A sixth-century tombstone on Tresco is now incorporated into the later priory church on the island. But early Christians in the islands had a tough time. From 780 onwards Viking raiders became the scourge of Atlantic seaboard communities and in 993 were reputed to have taken Scilly as a base.

Not long after the Norman Conquest of England, Scilly came directly under the rule of the new Crown. Surprisingly, no mention of the islands is directly made in their Domesday Book. By the time Henry I came to the throne in 1100, the problem

of sporadic Viking raids and pirates based in the islands probably spurred the granting of its rule to a monk from Tavistock Abbey in Devon.

The Duchy of Cornwall was established in 1337, when the Black Prince was granted the title of Duke. In a ledger dating to that year, Scilly was listed under foreign rents. The payment was 300 Puffin or 6s 8d. Apart from the fact that it is the first written record of the Puffin, it suggests that they may have been much more prolific than they are now. But further investigation reveals that the rent was usually settled in cash. So Puffins were obviously highly valued. At that time the bird was given special status on the menu: it was considered a fish rather than fowl, so could be eaten during Lent. Their feathers were also sought after. Yet half a century later, although the monetary value for the islands had not changed, the exchange rate for Puffin had increased by 600 per cent to just fifty birds.

For the next 400 years, England's wars and the islands' strategic importance at

Poppy and Corn Marigold

the entrance to the Western Approaches made life miserable for the islanders. It is thought that the final inundations by the sea occurred during this time and split Scilly into a series of smaller islands with sheltered anchorages between. Hidden coves and deserted isles, far from any protective naval force, offered a convenient retreat for pirates and privateers, enemy ships and fugitives. The islands developed a bad reputation as a lair for enemies of the crown. Thomas Seymour bought them in 1547, but after his execution for treachery, the Godolphin family began a rule of the islands which was to last for a remarkable 282 years. It only ended when Scilly was brought under the direct control of the Duchy again in 1831.

Because of the strategic importance of Scilly, the islanders' lives were precarious. Wars and disputes often turned subsistence survival to poverty and famine. Some islanders tried tin mining, but smuggling, wrecking and piloting seemed to be more profitable. In 1684 the production of soda ash from seaweed began, for the manufacture of soap, glass and bleach on the mainland, and lasted for nearly a century and a half. People scavenging the shores for seaweed must have had an impact on wildlife.

Then in 1879 a new industry took root. By all accounts, flower farming in Scilly began almost by accident. A vegetable grower on St Mary's added a few flowers to the crops he regularly sent to Covent Garden in London. But its real potential was realised and greatly expanded by Augustus Smith's nephew, T. A. Dorrien-Smith on Tresco, who introduced many different types of flower bulbs. So a new way of life soon blossomed across the islands. Flower cultivation also brought in more visitors to see the fields in bloom and a more lucrative business was born – tourism.

The advent of flower farming brought a new-found economic stability. The varieties of Narcissus cultivated in the islands once commonly grew only much further south in Europe. The origin of the first bulbs is unknown, but varieties like the 'Scilly White', a variety of the multi-stemmed 'Tazettas', were to be found wherever islanders lived. They grew wild beside cottage doors and in hedgerows, long before they were a cash crop. One suggestion is that the bulbs came to the islands with Benedictine monks from the south of France. It was even once said that wherever the monks trod, the flowers grew. Others claim that bulbs were used as barter by French fishermen. However, what is known is that from 1834 Augustus Smith was the Lord Proprietor of the islands and he was a keen collector of rare plants. He brought back many plants from his various trips to the Mediterranean.

Yet it seems that wherever cultivated flowers grow, so do wild plants. Whatever the origin of the bulbs, for a century and a half the flower farmers of Scilly have inadvertently created a remarkable and often stunningly beautiful landscape of wild flowers in their wake. They call them weeds, for that is exactly what they are – plants growing where they are not wanted. Elsewhere in England intensive farming and the widespread use of powerful herbicides have destroyed much of the country's native arable weeds. At least here in Scilly many still thrive, particularly Corn Marigold, Poppy and Corn Spurrey, creating a last vestige of old England.

Winter is the busiest time for the flower farmer, when Narcissi are picked and packed, yet fraught with problems when despatch to the mainland is delayed by bad weather. During the other half of the year, the fields are left fallow. Fortunately for wild-flower enthusiasts, most of the islands' farmers seem unworried by weed cover. Many of the wild flowers that grow are unusual and sometimes very rare.

Every few years the cultivated bulbs are lifted and carefully cleaned. Old and rotten ones are discarded, new ones replanted in their place. The progress of the tractor lifting the bulbs from the ground exposes a feast of worms and grubs. This heralds a feeding frenzy of Gulls, Blackbirds, Song Thrushes and other birds. The timing is mutually beneficial. Warm dry soil makes lifting bulbs easier for the farmer and provides an important source of food for breeding and newly fledged birds. In summer, long after the last of the cultivated flowers have died down and weeds set seed, the fields are cleared to reduce the risk of pests and disease damaging future crops.

During this process a chance discovery revolutionised the islands' fortunes. It was found that if a field containing 'Tazettas' was burnt while bulbs lay underground, they bloomed a few weeks earlier than normal. If it is burnt again, or the soil just exposed to smoke, perhaps three times, the bulbs could be forced to flower several weeks ahead of mainland competition. Coupled with the islands' famously mild winter temperatures, this gives the flower industry in Scilly a real head start. In the past, the burning was done with hay or straw but now propane gas burners roar in the fields. Remarkably the magic seems to come from the heat and smoke. It was a mystery for many years, but the answer is surprisingly simple. Daffodils need cooler conditions and do not respond. But 'Soleil d'Or' and other 'Tazettas' evolved in the Mediterranean where bush fires are common. If these plants shed their seed on ground stripped bare by burning, it gives the young growth a better chance to establish and form a new bulb before other plants can compete. We now know that smoke can contain a plant hormone and possibly other chemicals which trigger this response. An added bonus for some rare wild flowers is that fire also destroys more common weeds whilst allowing the winter-growing varieties to thrive.

Narcissi are not the only flowers to be grown in Scilly. Some cultivated varieties have now become weeds. Wild Gladiolus is known locally as Whistling Jacks because children use the leaves to blow a tune. The plants produce spikes of flamboyant dark red-purple flowers in May. Other former crops now growing wild include the Rosy Garlic and Ixia, particularly on St Mary's and St Martin's.

CLIMATE

The south-west of England enjoys the mildest climate in Britain. Bathed in warm prevailing winds from the Atlantic and ocean currents generated by the tropical Gulf Stream, the south-western peninsula is blessed with a plentiful supply of rain. Most of the moisture falls on the mainland, in the west on the highest ground.

On average the Isles of Scilly only receive between 850 and 900mm of rain each year, a little less than coastal areas on the nearby mainland. The sunshine record is among the highest in the UK, but temperatures are seldom very high. Wind is a major factor; the islands are low-lying and afford little protection against storms, although islands always offer shelter in their lee. The prevailing winds are from the south-west, and Scilly has another claim to fame: the Western Rocks are rated among the most exposed shores in the British Isles.

As a nation Britain enjoys an oceanic climate, while the Isles of Scilly are blessed by an extreme Atlantic form. Average temperatures usually vary by less than 9°C. Summers in the islands are seldom very hot, nor winters very cold. Frosts are rare, and snow even rarer. When snowfalls occur the schools have even been known to close, not because of its severity but so that pupils can enjoy a winter experience that many on the mainland take for granted.

Whistling Jacks

Wild Highlights

Whether you live in the islands or just visit for holidays, every season in Scilly has its wild highlights. Some plants and animals can be found nowhere else in Britain, others are much easier to see here. The islands contain a staggering 78 nationally rare plants and animals, and that does not include the marine life. What follows is my recommendation from personal experience, but you may also discover some of your very own.

SPRING

• Bulb-field flowers, both cultivated and wild

• **Scilly Bee** foraging among early flowers

• **Scilly Shrews** hunting among the boulders and seaweed at the top of a beach

• Migrant birds – quality not quantity, but several interesting birds usually turn up in spring

• **Puja plants** flower in late spring and early summer in the Abbey Gardens, Tresco

SUMMER

• **Swimming with seals** in the Eastern Isles or watching them at close quarters from a boat

• **Seabird colonies** on Samson and Western Rocks

• **Puffins** fly close to a boat off Annet

Scilly Bee; Grey Seal pup

- Sitting among **Sea Pinks** and just listening to the sea and birds

- **Giant Echium** or 'rocket plants' in many island gardens

- Rafts of **Manx Shearwater** can be seen in mid-summer at sunset between St Agnes and Annet

- **Stick insects** in the Abbey Gardens, Tresco

- The Western Isles on a calm day – or if you are a good sailor, in a heavy sea

- Paddling in the shallows on an uninhabited isle, watched by seals and seabirds

AUTUMN

- **Song Thrushes** hopping around your feet

- Migrant birds in October the main month for birding

- Watching waves in a Force 8 gale lashing the coast at Hell Bay

WINTER

- Bulb fields busy with pickers; they can look glorious in late winter.

- **Great Northern Divers** hiding in sheltered coves

- Peace and quiet

Song Thrush; Hell Bay

The Islands

All the main islands have beautiful, safe beaches, as well as good walking along lanes and tracks. On the off-islands and across the nature reserves, these trails are maintained by the Isles of Scilly Wildlife Trust, a registered charity with limited means. They do their best to keep the tracks, which are their responsibility, open and passable, but they can only do so with your help and support.

While bicycles are available on the bigger islands, only St Mary's has cars for hire. Otherwise walk or travel by boat – nowhere is far away in Scilly! All the main islands run boat trips to see the wildlife of the islands. While faster boats can cover more islands, they do not give you much time to enjoy the scenery and wildlife. St Mary's probably offers the widest choice of boat trips around the islands, but all inhabited islands are well served by their own boatmen. The skippers are knowledgeable, and also famed for their sense of humour.

TRAVEL TIPS

July and August are the peak holiday months, but even then the islands can hardly be described as crowded, as accommodation is limited. The trick is either to book early or try the Isles of Scilly Travel Centre for late cancellations. If you are a keen birdwatcher, then the spring and autumn migrations of birds can bring surprises by the hour. The first week of October is the best time for twitching, with rare vagrant birds from North America and Asia seen every year.

Walking is the best way to explore the islands; even the biggest can be circumnavigated comfortably in a couple of hours. There are three ways to reach the islands: by boat aboard *The Scillonian*; by helicopter from Penzance; or by Skybus plane, with services from Land's End, Exeter, Bristol and Southampton.

Men-a-vaur from St Helen's

A QUICK GUIDE TO THE ISLANDS

ST MARY'S
Bulb-field flowers, both cultivated and wild, are best throughout spring and even into early summer; also has some of the best examples of Neolithic tombs in Britain.

TRESCO
Beautiful beaches and dunes, primeval waved heathland, and the Abbey Gardens are worth visiting any time of the year. Remember spring starts early in Scilly. Watch for birds sipping nectar from exotic blooms like the Puja and Metrosideros in June. Offshore sandy shallows dry out at low-water springs, eel grass beds abundant.

ST MARTIN'S
Beautiful fine sandy beaches, as elsewhere in Scilly; Great Bay is magnificent. Look out for the rare St Martin's Ant on the east end heathlands.

ST AGNES AND GUGH
Summer Gull colonies on Gugh. St Agnes has most south-westerly freshwater pool in Britain. Stronghold of the Scilly Bee.

BRYHER
Hell Bay with a big Atlantic ocean swell is very impressive, especially in a storm. Look also for Dwarf Pansy around Rushy Bay, especially in April and May.

SAMSON
The largest uninhabited island in the archipelago contains many interesting historic features, as well as a large seagull colony in summer.

ANNET
Landing is not permitted on the bird sanctuary but boat trips provide the best views of the seabirds, especially Puffins.

ST HELEN'S
Some Puffin and Kittiwake, along with larger Gulls. Can be closed during bird breeding season.

TEAN
Delightful uninhabited island. The Meadow Brown and Blue butterflies are island specialities, and the Scilly Bee may feed from Foxgloves in June. Can be closed during seabird breeding season.

MEN-A-VAUR
Impressive rock stack, the best seabird colony for Auks.

EASTERN ISLES
Normally sheltered from south-westerly winds, seals bask on the rocks at low water.

WESTERN ROCKS
For breeding seals in August and September, seabirds throughout summer. Not for the faint-hearted unless it is very calm, but the boatmen know best.

St Mary's

The largest island in the archipelago is home to around three-quarters of the 2,000 or so people who live in Scilly. It also supports the busy main harbour and modern little airport. Apart from helicopter flights direct to Tresco, all ferry and air service links with the mainland arrive on St Mary's. Hugh Town is by far the biggest island community but it is still only the size of a village. This is the economic centre of the islands and contains all the basic facilities of a small town, with a selection of shops, restaurants and bars. Some excellent hotels, guest houses and self-catering accommodation are scattered across the island. Regular boat services from the harbour make travel between the islands easy and enjoyable. During the holiday season extra trips are also available to the outer islands to see thriving communities of seabirds and seals.

At its widest points, St Mary's is just 2¾ miles by 1¼ miles across. There are many fine coastal and country views, as well as some impressive archaeology. Prehistoric tombs, villages and forts are a major feature, and well worth taking the time to explore. The design of some of the Bronze Age graves in Scilly is unique and St Mary's has some of the most impressive and best preserved archaeological sites. The Giant's Tomb on Porth Hellick Down and Bant's Carn entrance grave on Halangy Down are both worth a visit. So too is the Iron Age village below Bant's Carn.

Being the largest island there are also places inland where you cannot see or even hear the sea, which is very unusual for Scilly. However, the biggest difference noticed by visitors is transport. Compared with the off-islands, where tractors are often the only motorised vehicles, cars and buses are becoming increasingly common on St Mary's winding roads.

Much of St Mary's is cultivated for flowers or early potatoes in a mosaic of tiny fields. High hedgerows protect the crops from salt-laden winds, where a variety of Daffodils and other Narcissi grow. The bulbs are forced to bloom early. Flower picking begins in October for London markets, and continues throughout the winter months. By the end of February flower prices fall and the harvest slows. Then St Mary's fields turn to shades of gold; the bulb fields are often rich in arable weeds.

The island boasts three Sites of Special Scientific Interest and two nature trails at Lower and Higher Moors, which are managed by the Isles of Scilly Wildlife Trust. All are joined by the coastal footpath. Although it is easy to circumnavigate St Mary's in a single day, it is far better to enjoy the island at a slower pace and explore the many attractive coves and coastal heathlands at leisure. The five-mile round island walk can take three to four hours. Taking a bus to the north end and walking back to Hugh Town is another popular option.

Woodland is scarce in Scilly. The only substantial trees that seem to do well on St Mary's are the native **Cornish Elm** and imported **Monterey Pine**. The Elm is mainly confined to the most sheltered side of The Garrison, overlooking Porthcressa Bay and on the Higher Moors trail between Porth Hellick and Holy Vale. The valley here is very sheltered with a tangibly mild microclimate. This feeling is confirmed by the lushness of exotic foliage bursting from gardens at the top of the vale. While

Port Thomas, St Mary's, in gale force winds

ST MARY'S

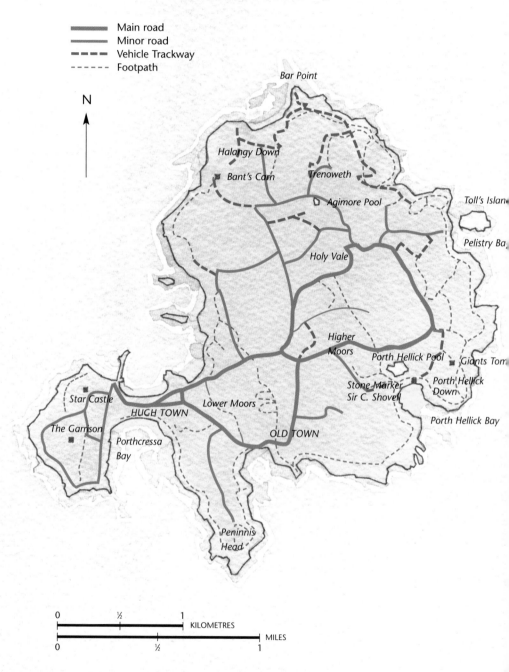

Main road
Minor road
Vehicle Trackway
Footpath

N

Bar Point

Halangy Down

Bant's Carn

Trenoweth

Agimore Pool

Toll's Island

Pelistry Bay

Holy Vale

Higher
Moors

Porth Hellick Pool

Giants Tomb

Star Castle

Stone Marker
Sir C. Shovell

Porth Hellick
Down

The Garrison

HUGH TOWN

Lower Moors

OLD TOWN

Porth Hellick Bay

Porthcressa
Bay

Peninnis
Head

0   ½   1
                              KILOMETRES
0   ½   1
                              MILES

the Monterey Pine was planted as a front-line shelter belt against the wind, the elms do best in sheltered hedgerows. Since the ravages of Dutch Elm disease on the mainland this is one of the few places in Britain where you can still walk beneath the leafy boughs of elm trees.

Higher Moors and Lower Moors

These moors are both fed by small streams and groundwater from surrounding higher areas. The water spreads over the valley floor forming a patchwork of pools, mire and scrub of willow and alder. They are vital feeding and breeding places for resident wildlife, as well as attracting large numbers of migrant, summer and winter visiting birds, including **Mallard**, **Gadwall**, **Teal**, **Moorhen**, **Coot** and **Warblers**.

They are also valuable as a window on the past. The ancient peat deposits of these wetlands preserve plant pollen well and this has helped to shape our knowledge of the island's changing vegetation over thousands of years.

These Nature Reserves consist mainly of wetlands where **Common Reed** crowds out other vegetation, and the trails are fringed by **Grey Willow** with sentinel-like growths of **Royal Fern** and **Greater Tussock-sedge**. **Southern Marsh Orchid** and **Yellow Flag Iris** can also be seen here during early summer.

Porth Hellick Bay

This is one of the most attractive sheltered coves in the island, not only for walkers but also for a delightful little bird – the **Ringed Plover**. A good view of the beach during the Plover's breeding season in early summer can be gained from a stone marker on the spot where the body of Admiral Sir Cloudsley Shovell was found in 1707. But take care when walking on the beach, as the **Ringed Plover** makes just a scrape and lays her well camouflaged eggs directly on the sand.

Overleaf: Halangy Down ancient village

Holy Vale Nature Trail

Porth Hellick Pool

Porth Hellick Pool is the largest area of open water on St Mary's and is separated from the sea by a sand and shingle bar. On the seaward side only plants that can endure high levels of salt can survive, such as **Sea Rush, Scentless Mayweed** and **Yellow horned Poppy**. While on the bar itself the dominant native growth is **Sea Sandwort** with some **Sea Kale** but thick mats of an alien invader cover its crest. Running along the landward side of the ridge the fleshy-leaved **Hottentot Fig** runs riot.

A small stream flowing from Holy Vale into the Pool is the only stream of any size in Scilly. Although the pool itself contains freshwater, some more salt-enduring plants can be found, including **Brackish Water-crowfoot, Sea Milkwort, Sea Club-rush** and **Saltmarsh Rush**. The Pool is fringed with **Common Reed** backed by **Grey Willow** with a scattering of **Bulrush**. The surrounding waterlogged soils support some more typical wetland species such as **Yellow Iris, Soft Rush, Lesser Spearwort, Water Mint, Gypsywort, Hemlock Water-dropwort** and **Ragged Robin**. Impressive stands of **Royal Fern, Greater Tussock-sedge** and **Southern Marsh Orchid** can also be seen, mainly flanking the path. **Star Sedge, Bog Stitchwort, Bog Pondweed** and **Bog Pimpernel** reveal the more acidic boggy areas.

The Pool and surrounding reed beds are important for breeding and migrant birds, including **Mallard, Gadwall, Teal, Coot, Moorhen** and **Sedge Warbler**. The site also provides valuable food and shelter for other wintering birds and regularly attracts many rare vagrants.

Porth Hellick Pool

Agimore Pool
Near Trenoweth, this pool is small but is easily accessible and contains some interesting plants. It also sometimes attracts rare birds during spring and autumn migration so is always worth a good look.

Peninnis Head
On the south side of St Mary's, this area is well known for its spectacular smooth granite outcrop. Howling east or southerly gales carry salt spray far inland, and it is partly for this reason that the cliff headlands here, as elsewhere in Scilly, consist mainly of salt-tolerant maritime heath and grasses along with some scrub in more sheltered parts. The other reason is its prehistoric past. At the peak of the ice ages, St Mary's lay on the southernmost limit of the great ice sheet that once covered most of the British Isles. Standing on Peninnis Head at that time the scene would have been remarkable. Looking north, a vast cliff of crumbling ice would have stretched across the horizon from east to west.

While the north coast of St Mary's reveals glaciated bedrock and 'head' deposits, the thin-soiled southern headlands are more exposed to wind and sea. This has led to the formation of so-called 'waved' heathland. It is a feature of many of the most exposed south-west cliffs but more easily accessible here on St Mary's. Peninnis Head is a popular destination for an evening stroll in summer, and it is always worth looking out for oceanic seabirds offshore such as **Gannet** or **Manx Shearwater**.

The Garrison
This impressive fortification has breathtaking views over the islands, especially from the strategically placed Star Castle. Building started in 1593 as a response to the threat of further invasion after the ill-fated Spanish Armada just five years before. The castle was the last of a defensive chain of similar fortifications that stretched along England's channel shore from Kent to Cornwall.

The following two centuries saw the construction of a substantial outer wall forming a secure ring around the island. The main coastal footpath closely follows the line of the wall and provides a relatively easy walk with some fine coastal views. Watch out for passing seabirds, as well as **Rock Pipit** and **Wheatear** during the summer months.

Tooth Rock on Peninnis Head

Old Town

Old Town is delightful. Its beach is well sheltered from all but an easterly wind, in a perfect crescent shape with fine white sand, and is easy to reach. Formerly known as Porthennor, this was the original early medieval settlement established when Scilly was probably still one substantial island. Then it would have been possible to walk to St Martin's via Samson, Bryher, Tresco, St Helen's and Tean. Hardly anything now survives of the original thirteenth-century castle, but a large granite fish salting trough can still be seen on the northern side. At low tide the bay offers good opportunities for exploring rock pools for marine life and at high tide for snorkelling.

Pelistry Bay

Sheltered from the prevailing south-westerly winds with lovely views of the Eastern Isles and St Martin's, Pelistry Bay is a wonderfully secluded cove with a fine beach and its very own little island, Tolls Island, which can only be reached and explored at low tide. Look out for the remains of a seventeenth-century fort, and enjoy snorkelling among the **Kelp** and resident seals. Outside the summer season the bay can also attract **Sea Ducks** and occasional **Divers**. Exploring the coastline here on horseback from the nearby riding centre is a great way to see the area.

Bar Point

On the island's north coast is an oasis of white sand dunes backing the beach with an interesting flora typical of such places. It can only be reached by the scenic coastal footpath, which provides magnificent views across to the islands of St Martin's and Tresco.

St Mary's Old Town   *Oil Beetle in Hottentot Fig*
Overleaf: Peninnis Head in a gale

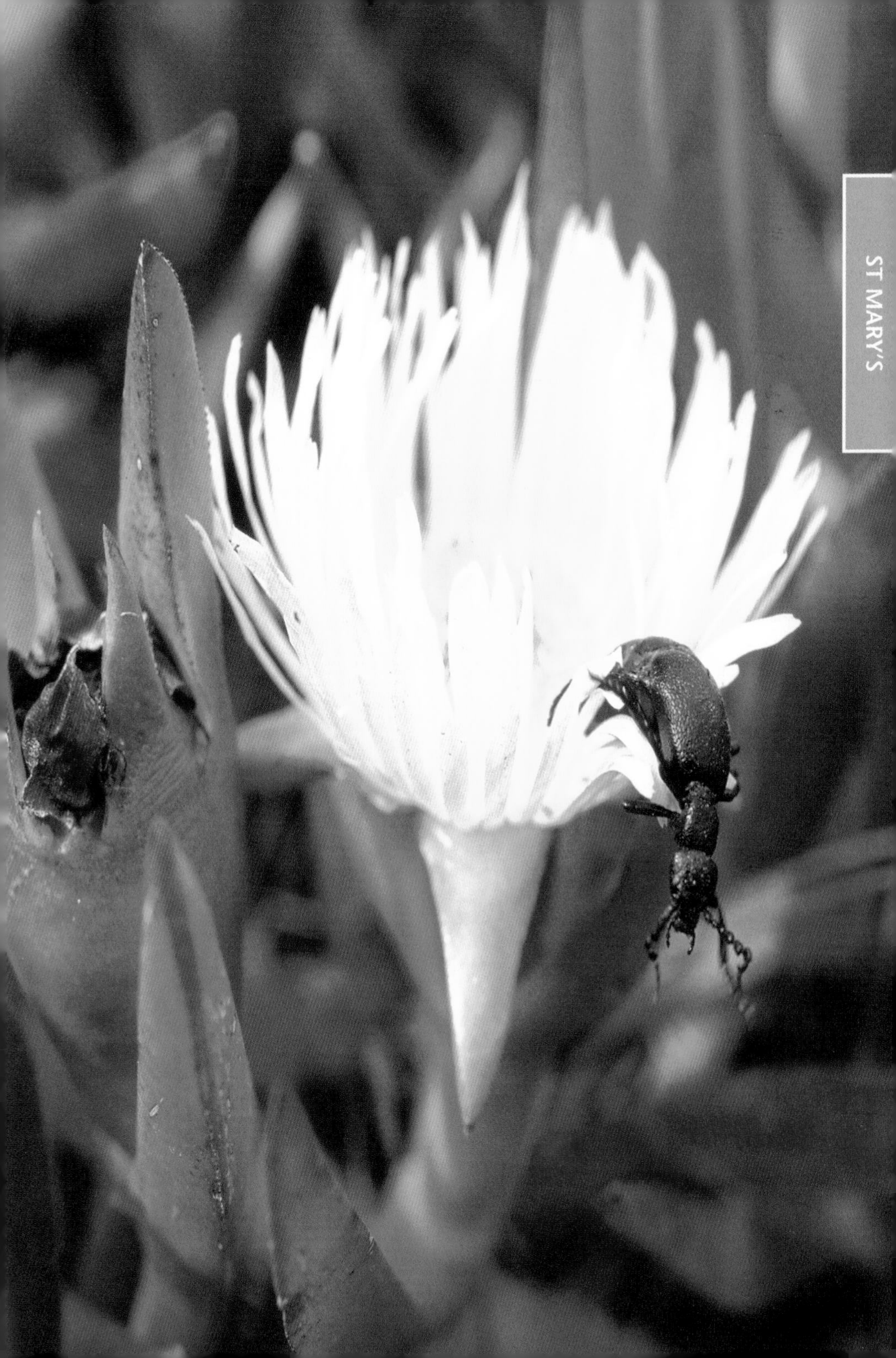

Tresco

Tresco is unique in Scilly. No other island offers such a contrast in scenery, from windswept primeval headlands through sheltered bulb fields and sensational subtropical gardens to beautiful dune-backed beaches. The contrast between the wind-buffeted western cliffs and the shelter of the Abbey Gardens in particular is extraordinary. It can take less than an hour to stroll from a bracing Atlantic view to the peace and serenity of one of the world's most famous gardens. And there is another difference: Tresco is leased from the Duchy of Cornwall by Robert Dorrien-Smith, whose family first came to Scilly over 170 years ago.

In 1834 Augustus Smith left his home in Hertfordshire to take up residence in the islands. He became the leaseholder of Scilly with the title of Lord Proprietor. He chose Tresco as his base and built his home close to the ruins of the twelfth-century abbey. What he discovered on the islands must have shocked him. Poverty and subsistence living seemed to be a way of life for many islanders, so he set about introducing new industries and is credited with establishing new agricultural practices, developing flower farming and even tourism. He financed the building of schools and revitalised the island economy. His vision also created the now world-famous subtropical Abbey Gardens.

Tresco Abbey Gardens

The new Tresco Abbey was situated on a rocky outcrop, and the granite for its construction was quarried on site. Augustus Smith began the garden immediately after completing the house. A series of walled enclosures around the old ruin formed the first garden but any further development of terracing the treeless south facing slope would require more than just walls to protect them from Atlantic gales. What was needed was a windbreak on a grand scale. On the western side a shelter belt of trees was planted as the first line of defence, followed by ranks of evergreen hedges and walls. By 1855 the construction of a series of terraced paths linked by steps formed the basic structure. In the increasingly sheltered garden luxuriant displays of succulent and Mediterranean-style planting flourished in the Scillonian sun.

The impressive garden design laid down by Augustus Smith was continued by his heirs. Each added their own elements of inspiration through trial and error. Plants were gathered from around the globe with a later emphasis on flowers and shrubs from South African, Australia and New Zealand. The result is the most extraordinary and beautiful subtropical growth to be found anywhere in England. Despite the island's relative inaccessibility, greatly ameliorated by the addition of its own heliport, Tresco Abbey Gardens now has a world-class reputation. It is a garden of such international renown that the world now beats a path to its door and its wildlife is no less exceptional.

Surrounded by warm water currents emanating from the Gulf Stream and protected from the worst of the wind by its shelterbelt of conifers and tall evergreen hedges, the climate inside this garden is subtropical. Even in midwinter more than

Tresco Abbey and gardens

TRESCO

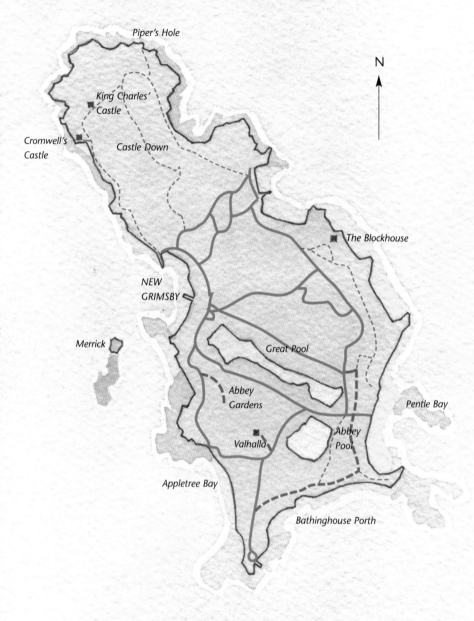

Piper's Hole

King Charles' Castle

Cromwell's Castle

Castle Down

N

The Blockhouse

NEW GRIMSBY

Merrick

Great Pool

Abbey Gardens

Pentle Bay

Valhalla

Abbey Pool

Appletree Bay

Bathinghouse Porth

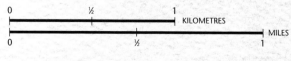

| 0 | ½ | 1 |
KILOMETRES

| 0 | ½ | 1 |
MILES

300 plants will be in flower. The garden blooms with a bewildering variety of exotic plants, many species of which survive and flower here as nowhere else in Britain and they come from far and wide. These gardens are home to plants from eighty countries, ranging from the Mediterranean to South America, as well as the gardens' 'specialities', South Africa to Australia and New Zealand. Not many places can offer a world tour in less than 17 acres!

This variety of flowers not only provides a wonderful display but also offers wildlife some remarkable opportunities. Here, not only are plants exotic but aliens also stalk the undergrowth.

One of the most dramatic plants to flower in the Abbey Gardens is a native of the high Andes Mountains in Chile. The **Puja** plant produces huge spikes bearing large, waxy jade-green flowers in early summer. Their stamens are thick with pollen, which can be bright yellow or even orange, and the flowers brim with sweet nectar. Large numbers of ants and other insects are attracted to the sticky feast. So too are birds. In its native mountains, the plant is pollinated by the heads of nectar-sipping birds. Here in Scilly that job is done by **Starlings** and **Blackbirds**. The plant even provides handy perches for the birds to reach the flowers, spiralling up the stem. It seems, however, that some birds are just as keen to eat the insects attracted by the nectar. So some Tresco birds get a bonus while pollinating the Puja flower – a sugar-

Puja flower   *Overleaf: Metrosideros – Abbey Gardens*

dipped, protein-filled snack. So profuse is the pollen production that the garden birds often develop a yellow or golden cap, resulting in a flurry of claims from garden visitors of having seen some very exotic birds.

The Puja also attracts other, smaller birds for a different reason. In dry weather **Sparrows** and **Chaffinches** have learned to visit the large flowers after a shower of rain. The waxy, upward facing blooms fill with water and the birds are quick to quench their thirst from these ready-sweetened cups.

House Sparrows also sip nectar from other plants. **Red Hot Pokers** are a favourite target but their antics on these plants are not welcomed by the gardener. They have a rather short stubby bill, adapted for eating seed and not really suitable for reaching down the throat of long tubular blooms. So they have learnt to be devious: they peck a hole in the base of the flower or simply rip the bloom apart.

The gardens also contain a collection of fascinating ancient artefacts and salvaged remnants of some of Scilly's most famous shipwrecks. Valhalla is situated on the edge of the garden and shelters a magnificent collection of colourful ship's figureheads, several in remarkably good condition. It also displays some well-preserved cannons, remounted on wooden carriages. Among the most interesting artefacts, however, are a Bronze Age holed rock, an inscribed Romano-British stone, and a Roman shrine which depicts a dagger and an axe, perhaps indicating that it was a sacrificial altar.

New Grimbsy

Tresco has played an important part in the history of the islands. New Grimsby harbour is a safe anchorage, as popular with visiting yachts today as it was in times past. Protected from gales by the high ground either side of the channel dividing Tresco from Bryher, the seabed here offers good holding for anchors. The strategic importance of the place can be seen from the forts built for its protection. King Charles' Castle and the Blockhouse were constructed around 1550 to defend the islands against Spanish and French attack. In 1648, after the end of the English Civil War, Scilly briefly joined the uprising against Cromwell's Parliament. Pirates and privateers preying on trading ships in the English Channel became regular visitors, to such extent that the Dutch declared war on the islands and sent an invasion fleet. Alarmed at the potential loss of Scilly, the English Parliament sent its own forces to defeat the Dutch. A few years later Cromwell's Castle was built, replacing King Charles' in a better position, closer to the water.

Evidence of earlier settlements can also be discovered on Tresco. Submerged hut circles and field walls may be found in Bathinghouse Porth and more walling can be seen at the south end of Pentle Bay. The visibility of both, however, is dependent on the level of sand.

Castle Down

At the northern end of the island lies this exposed heathland, just 35 metres above sea level. A superb example of waved heath, it covers most of the central part of this thin-soiled, windswept terrain. **Bell Heather** and **Ling** dominate, along with **Western Gorse**. Few other plants can endure the extremely windy conditions up here so **bracken** and **bramble** are confined to more sheltered pockets of deeper soil. **Lichens** are among Castle Down's most important plants, and some 45 different species have been identified so far, including one of the rarest oceanic heathland species, **Coralloid Rosette-lichen**, of which Scilly is the only known European location. Other *Heterodermia* lichens found here occur elsewhere only on the most windswept coasts of Brittany and the Channel Islands.

Common Tern are the most notable birds to have bred on Castle Down in the past, and some nesting **Ringed Plover** have also been reported.

Piper's Hole
A small cave on the north-eastern side of the island, formed in the raised-beach deposit below Castle Down's cliff, is known as Piper's Hole. Several rare cave-living plants abd animals have been discovered here, at least two of which are new to the British Isles. Access to the caves is at best difficult and at worst dangerous. Extreme care must be taken if a visit is planned.

Appletree Bay and Pentle Bay
On the more sheltered southern end of Tresco, these bays form the biggest sand-dune system in Scilly. Down on the shore above the strandline grow **Sea Spurge**, **Sea Rocket** and **Sea Purslane**, while higher up the nationally rare **Shore Dock** can be found. **Marram Grass** dominates the low dunes where **Sea Stork's-bill**, **Sand Sedge**, **Bird's-foot Trefoil**, **Portland Spurge** and **Suffocated Clover** can also be seen. Two other plants commonly found here are rare on the mainland: **Babington's Leek** and

Common Tern

Balm-leaved Figwort make these dunes especially important.

Several escaped garden plants have also become established. Most memorable are the exotic bright blue **Agapanthus**. Native to South Africa, they thrive in Tresco's southern dunes, flowering through late summer.

Heading inshore, **Bramble** and **Bracken** have begun to invade the deeper soil areas, before the sand dunes merge into the thin-soiled, lichen-rich heathland. Several nationally rare lichen can be found here, including **Ciliate Strapwort** and two **Lungworts** which in Scilly grow on heather. On the mainland these lichen can only be found growing on deciduous trees. A few liverworts which are rare on the mainland can also be discovered here: *Lophocolea semiteres* and *Fossombronia foveolata*.

Common Terns once regularly bred on these dunes, but they are unpredictable birds when it comes to breeding, and are easily disturbed by people. They now seem to have moved to islands just offshore such as Merrick and other small rocky islets. Tresco's beaches and rocky headlands also attract **Oystercatchers** and **Ringed Plover**, and both have been known to breed on these southern shores.

Great Pool

Great Pool is the largest body of freshwater in Scilly with a developing reed swamp. It is protected from the sea by a narrow sand bank at Abbey Farm in the west, with a more extensive dune system at its eastern end. The build-up of alluvium, silt and peat has produced a shallow lake with average nutrient levels, good for a range of wetland-loving birds and plants. In the shallows some rare **Brackish Water-crow-foot**, along with **Fennel Pondweed** and **Water-milfoil** grow. **Common Reed** forms wide growths around most of the water margin, while **Bulrush** is more evident at the southern end. In the waterlogged wetlands **Royal Fern**, **Soft Rush** and **Tubular Water-dropwort** can be seen. Along the northern edge **Grey Willow** grows densely along with **Yellow Iris** and **Marsh Pennywort**. In the drier parts **Creeping Buttercup**, **Lesser Celandine**, **Stinking Iris**, **Babington's Leek** and **Balm-leaved Figwort** can all be found.

In a place surrounded by the sea, freshwater wetlands are an important and rare breeding area for wildfowl such as **Mute Swan**, **Gadwall** and **Mallard**, as well as many other birds. **Sedge Warbler**, **Reed Warbler** and **Water Rail** can all be seen during the breeding season, while in winter good numbers of **Wigeon** and **Teal** with **Shoveler**, **Tufted Duck**, **Mallard**, **Gadwell** and **Pochard** are regular visitors. Great Pool is always worth checking out during spring and autumn migration time, as rare vagrants often turn up from North America.

Abbey Pool

This is much smaller, but no less popular with some birds, especially wildfowl and waders.

Tresco Channel and Bryher

St Martin's

One of the most attractive and picturesque inhabited islands, St Martin's lies on the north-eastern edge of the archipelago and is renowned for its sweeping bays of fine white sand. Just over 1½ miles long by about 1 mile wide, it is the third-largest inhabited island in Scilly. There are only about thirty households on the island, with a resident population of around 100 people living in Higher Town, Middle Town and Lower Town.

The northern end faces the Atlantic with its wild coastline broken by rugged rocky outcrops and sandy coves. Both ends and the eastern half of the island are covered by heathland, while the southern shore has superb sandy beaches. The charming little hedge-boxed flower and vegetable fields are all on the sunny, south-west-facing slopes, where most of the settlements can be found.

St Martin's is rich in prehistoric remains. An alignment of entrance graves runs along the crest of Cruther's Hill, similar to those found on Samson and Gugh. A Bronze Age menhir has been repositioned to the south of Chapel Down and one of the few intact entrance graves found in Scilly was excavated at Knackyboy Carn.

The foundations of an early Christian chapel lie below the red-and-white-striped Daymark on Chapel Down. It was not unusual for religious houses to guide shipping with lights positioned on headlands. Many of the most prominent coastal headlands in the British Isles are named after saints, so the practice must have been widespread.

Wildlife
St Martin's contains several Sites of Special Scientific Interest and is particularly noted for its maritime plants and animals, geology and marine life.

Shore Life
The most important sand flats in Scilly lie just south-west of St Martin's. Exposed only at low water, they stretch from the hotel quay to Cruther's Point and extend offshore to some rocky outcrops known as Pigs, Moths and Round Rock Ledges. Tidal flows across these flats naturally grade the sand and gravel into distinct deposits, sometimes reshaping the shore and producing a rich variety of different habitats. The beach can vary from coarse to medium-sized sand grains, cobbles, boulders and solid reef. In the finest sand live burrowing **Heart Urchins** – bivalve molluscs – and marine worms often attract wading birds to feed.

One of the most curious features is that some marine creatures not usually found within the intertidal zone seem to thrive here. The **Sea Potato** normally prefers to live in areas that never dry out, and the **Sea-urchin** can be found just below mean low water. **Sand Hoppers** and sea snail such as the **Netted Dog Whelk** seem to thrive on these flats, and a rich variety of bivalve molluscs include **Razor Shells**, **Rayed Artemis** and **Thin Tellin**. Marine worms found here include **Lugworm**, **Ragworm** and **Sandworm** along with many other smaller relatives. Even **Sea Cucumber** is not uncommon. The rocky areas can form pools at low water where an amazing variety of marine creatures can be seen.

St Martin's with some of the Eastern Isles in the foreground

ST MARTIN'S

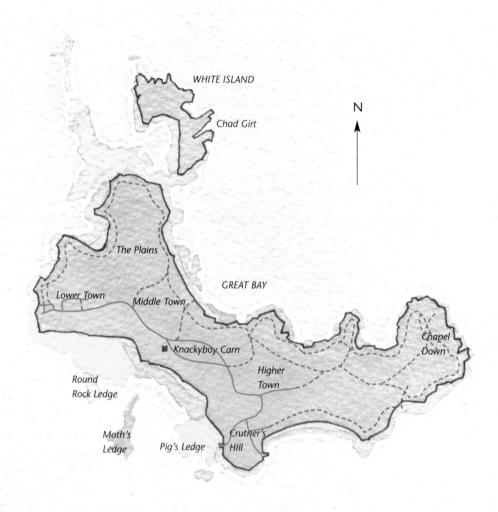

WHITE ISLAND

Chad Girt

N

The Plains

GREAT BAY

Lower Town

Middle Town

Knackyboy Carn

Chapel
Down

Round
Rock Ledge

Higher
Town

Moth's
Ledge

Pig's Ledge

Cruther's
Hill

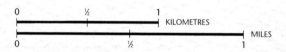

0   ½   1
KILOMETRES

0   ½   1
MILES

Chapel Down

At the eastern end of the island, Chapel Down rises to 35 metres high. Surrounded by steep cliffs, the plateau inland is covered by thin soil where waved heath has developed. Along the north-eastern coast the exposed cliffs reveal an interesting geology with glacial mud and gravel.

Bell Heather and **Ling**, along with low-growing **Western Gorse**, cover most of the high plateau along with **Common Bird's-foot Trefoil, English Stonecrop, Heath Bedstraw** and **Tormentil**. The nationally rare **Jointed Orange Bird's-foot** and interesting little **Hairy Bird's-foot Trefoil** also grow here. Towards the western end, **European Gorse** takes over and a small number of **Pignut** plants can be found.

Deeper soil covers the more sheltered northern slope and here **Bracken, Bramble** and **Honeysuckle** can form a tangled scrub by late summer. Coldwind Pit is wetter, and contains **Bristle Club-rush, Heath Grass** and **Marsh Pennywort**. Along the cliff edge the maritime grassland contains **Thrift, Sea Beet, Sorrel** and some **Buck's-horn Plantain**.

Below the Daymark some interesting lichens can be found, including a rare maritime species, the **Coralloid Rosette-lichen**.

The so-called **St Martin's Ant** was also discovered here, living under stones on the heathland.

The Plains and Great Bay

On the north side of the island Great Bay contains a spectacular east-facing beach backed by sand dunes. The strandline is always worth a look and many of the plants typical of such places grow here above the reach of high tide. **Sea Sandwort, Frosted Orache** and **Sea Rocket** are common. Amongst the **Marram** and **Sand Couch** in the dunes, **Sea Spurge, Portland Spurge** and **Sea Holly** can usually be

Bell Heather on St Martin's, with White Island beyond

found. Walking inland the rabbit grazed turf above the shore is rich in **Thrift, Red Fescue, Sea Storksbill** and **Eyebright**. Beyond lies heathland and denser growths of bramble and bracken. The bay is also a good place for breeding **Ringed Plover**.

White Island
On the north-eastern edge of the archipelago this small island is connected to St Martin's by a boulder-strewn causeway which is exposed at low tide. This is the only island where slate can still be found, along with some interesting and well-studied deposits of mud and mainly granite gravel spilled from glaciers up to 34,000 years ago. Today they are known as Chad Girt. Scientific researchers have been investigating the island for many years. Their findings have unearthed a remarkable sequence of prehistoric events. Like the chapters in a book, each layer contains important clues which help to tell the story of Scilly through time.

The island has a few entrance graves and several stone cairns, as well as a later kelp pit. Between the seventeenth and eighteenth centuries the Nance family began a cottage industry, burning seaweed to produce soda and potash which was then exported as a constituent for the making of glass and soap. The work must have been hard with little return.

There are also important areas of maritime heath and grassland, scrub and isolated cliffs with small colonies of nesting seabirds. The exposed upper parts are a fine example of waved heath. These thin-soiled exposed areas mainly support **Bell Heather** and **Ling** with **Western Gorse, Common Heath Bedstraw, Bird's-foot Trefoil** and **English Stonecrop**. In more sheltered places the deeper soils allow **Bramble** and **Bracken** to grow with some **Honeysuckle**. On the western side, along the coastal margin, the maritime grassland has good tufts of **Thrift** with **Red Fescue, Sea Beet, Common Scurvy Grass** and **Buck's-horn Plantain**.

Fulmar and **Kittiwake** nest in a few places, while **Herring Gull, Lesser Black-backed Gull** and **Great Black-backed Gull** and can be seen throughout the summer.

Honeysuckle   *Kittiwake at nest*

St Agnes and Gugh

The most westerly inhabited island is separated from St Mary's by a deep-water channel. St Agnes and Gugh must have been among the first islands to have lost their land link to the rest of the archipelago, perhaps over 1,000 years ago. They are the smallest and in many ways the most interesting of islands. Being the first to be isolated they have perhaps retained more of their Iron Age Celtic heritage. Wells and springs were considered by the Celts to be sacred portals to the underworld. So when Christianity first arrived they merely supplanted the pagan customs and converted their veneration of freshwater sources into 'holy' wells. One unique example survives as St Warna's Well on the west side of Wingletang Down. It is thought that an offering to this water goddess, unknown outside of St Agnes, may have enticed ships to wreck on the island. Certainly its excavation revealed many interesting small artefacts and over the centuries the spoils from wrecks have undoubtedly helped the island economy. When it comes to wrecks, St Agnes is in a league of its own – it can claim more ships than any other island in Scilly. But that hopefully has more to do with mistakes than magic; the island was after all the first landfall for sailing ships entering the English Channel on a westerly wind.

The island's danger to shipping later led to the construction of St Agnes's most obvious feature – a central white lighthouse. Today it is a landmark rather than a light. Standing 23 metres high, it was built in 1680 and is the oldest in Scilly. Originally fired by coal and later by oil, it lasted over two centuries before being superseded by a brighter, more powerful light at Peninnis Head on St Mary's. The original large fire basket is now on display in Tresco Abbey Gardens.

St Agnes offers some delightful walking past tiny bulb fields bursting with colourful wild flowers, and attractive little beaches. These shores are thought by many to be the most enticing of any on the islands. Cove Vean and The Bar are the most sheltered, while Periglis on the west coast offers an unrivalled view out to the Western Rocks and Atlantic Ocean beyond. The island has a timeless feel, no doubt reinforced by the evidence of past settlements. It has more than its fair share of prehistoric remains, including entrance graves and substantial Bronze Age standing stones. The best-known menhir is the Old Man of Gugh. Over 3,000 years ago the view from here would have been very different – looking north towards a single large island and east over a sandy cove nestled between Gugh and the high ground of Peninnis and The Garrison.

The Iron Age hut circles at Tol Tuppens on the north-western side of Gugh's 34-metre-high Kittern Hill can best be seen before summer growth buries them from view.

Gugh (in the foreground) and St Agnes

ST AGNES AND GUGH

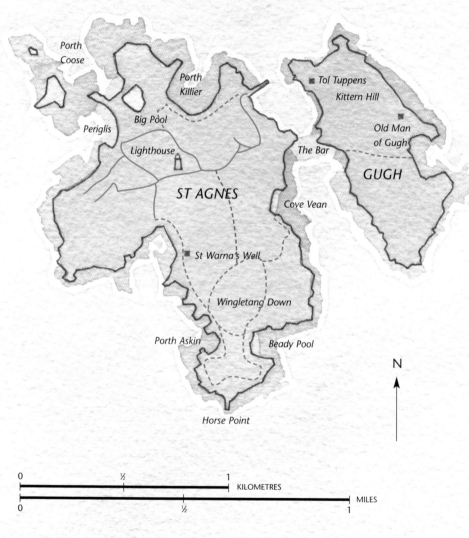

Porth
Coose

Porth
Killier

Big Pool

Periglis

Lighthouse

ST AGNES

Tol Tuppens

Kittern Hill

Old Man
of Gugh

The Bar

GUGH

Cove Vean

St Warna's Well

Wingletang Down

Porth Askin

Beady Pool

N

Horse Point

0   ½   1
                    KILOMETRES

0   ½   1
                                        MILES

St Agnes

The central area of St Agnes around the lighthouse is a tiny mosaic of fields. Each plot is surrounded by tall evergreen hedgerows, which not only filter the wind but provide important cover for small birds during spring and autumn migrations. So it is not surprising, considering its westerly position, that St Agnes boasts the longest bird list for Scilly, many of which are new to Britain and Europe. But birds are not the only winged travellers and the island's list of migrant moths is equally impressive.

Big Pool and Little Pool
These twin pools are the most westerly source of open freshwater in England, and **Fennel Pondweed** grows there. Separated from the sea by only a narrow shingle ridge and boulder beach, and drenched by salt spray, they are also sometimes reached by storm-driven waves in winter. This probably explains the presence of **Sea Clubrush** and **Saltmarsh Rush** around pool margins. More surprising is the presence of a thick layer of sand across their bottoms. Rather alarmingly this is thought to have been deposited by a tsunami in 1755 created by the terrible Lisbon earthquake over 1,000 miles away.

The nearby short wet grasslands contain many interesting and nationally rare plants, including **Suffocated** and **Western Clovers** and **Least Adder's Tongue**. The short turf also supports **Bristle Clubrush**, **Subterranean Clover**, **Chamomile** and **Autumn Lady's-tresses**. In the southern part **Early Meadow-grass** can also be found growing along the trackway across the drier grassland.

Big Pool on St Agnes

Shore Life

The beaches of Periglis, Porth Coose and Porth Killier have particularly fine growths of the large-leaved **Sea Kale** and smaller **Sea Radish**, often found in the same place as **Babington's** and **Frosted Orache**.

These shores can also be important for breeding **Ringed Plover**, while **Moorhen, Coot, Mallard** and **Gadwall** have all nested at Big Pool. **Mallard** also overwinter with flocks of wading birds such as **Sanderling, Turnstone, Curlew, Redshank, Grey Plover** and **Purple Sandpiper**.

Wingletang Down

This area is noted for its low-lying heathland, which is barely 20 metres above sea level. Its thin soil is littered with granite outcrops and well-weathered rocks. In places between Beady Pool and Porth Askin, wind-driven sand covers the granite bed. Much of the area has formed important waved heath with **Least Adder's-tongue** and **Jointed Orange Bird's-foot**. Only the occasional invasion of **Bracken** and **European Gorse** threatens to engulf them. Other plants to look out for include a tiny orchid, **Autumn Lady's-tresses**, as well as **Bristle Clubrush** and **Early Meadow-grass**.

At the back of Beady Pool, just on and above the strandline, **Sea Kale** and **Yellow Horned Poppy** can thrive, while at Horse Point the rare **Sea-milkwort** can be found. In the dune grasslands to the south the plant community is largely made up of **Portland Spurge, Sand Sedge, Sand Couch** and **Common Stork's-bill**.

Ringed Plover breed on the beaches, so it is important to watch where you tread, while **Oystercatchers** tend to keep to the upper shore. **Herring Gulls** can nest all along the north-west coast. There are also reports of **Storm Petrels** breeding in the more exposed boulder beaches on the west side.

Gugh

The island of Gugh is linked to St Agnes by a sand and shingle bar exposed at low tide. Waved heath covers much of the higher ground and a good number of **Jointed Orange Bird's-foot** occur in the lichen-rich southern part, which includes **Golden Hair-lichen** and **Lungwort**. On the northern edge and elsewhere around the coast, fine displays of **Thrift** grow in the maritime grasslands with some nationally rare **Early Meadow-grass** and **Least Adder's-tongue**. Another uncommon plant found here is the **Western Clover**.

At the eastern end of the Bar, wind-blown sand has formed into small dunes where **Sand Couch** and **Marram** rustle in the breeze. In the adjacent grasslands **Portland Spurge, Common Stork's-bill** and **Sand Sedge** thrive, and this is also the only known location for **Viper's Bugloss** in the islands. Inland, the central part of Gugh is covered by **Bracken** with some scattered **Balm-leaved Figwort**.

Three interesting invertebrates have also been discovered, a woodlouse, centipede and a rare moth – the **Kent Black Arches**. The most obvious seabird on Gugh is a colony of **Lesser Black-backed Gull** at the southern end. Good numbers of **Kittiwake** can now be found nesting on low cliffs on the north-eastern side. There are also records of **Ringed Plover, Storm Petrel** and **Manx Shearwater** nesting on the island.

Viper's Bugloss and Heather

Bryher

The smallest inhabited island in Scilly, Bryher is breathtaking in its beauty. It is also an island of great contrast. Standing on Shipman Head Down overlooking Hell Bay in a full-blown Atlantic gale is an experience not to be missed. Yet just a short walk away in the shelter of Tresco Channel, the same island can appear a haven of tranquillity. The bleakness of Bryher during the terrifying fury of a winter storm is so different from the calm of its summer face – indeed, so different it is hard to believe it is the same island. Yet even in midwinter the day after a storm, Bryher can bask under a blue sky, a picture of peace and wild serenity.

The greatest change to Scilly since ancient times is undoubtedly rising sea levels. In Green Bay, just south of Church Quay, the remains of a prehistoric stone wall can easily be seen on the beach. This is a tangible reminder that nothing in nature stands still. Partly buried, the large weed-covered granite boulder wall rises out of the tidal sand flats and seems to march up the beach as the tide retreats.

Shipman Head

The rocky headland itself is a difficult and dangerous place to reach, so should not be visited. Largely covered by waved heath, with **Bell Heather**, **Ling** and **Western Gorse**, its cliffs are an undisturbed haven for nesting seabirds. There are large colonies of **Kittiwake** and **Herring Gull** along with **Great** and **Lesser Black-backed Gulls**, **Razorbill**, **Shag** and **Storm Petrel**. Even **Ringed Plover** sometimes breed up on the heathland.

Shipman Head Down

This offers good views over the island and has an astonishing number of stone piles known as cairns; over 100 are visible and some are linked by old stone walls. A large number are thought

Hell Bay   *Bryher from Shipman Head Down*

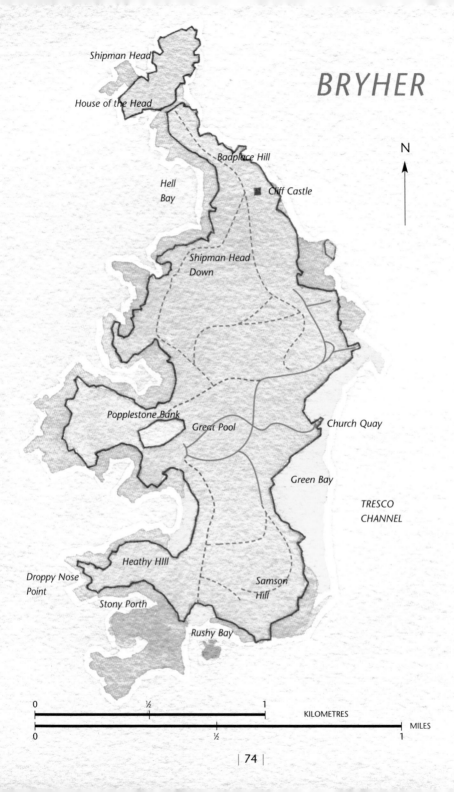

BRYHER

Shipman Head

House of the Head

Badplace Hill

Hell
Bay

Cliff Castle

N

Shipman Head
Down

Popplestone Bank

Great Pool

Church Quay

Green Bay

TRESCO
CHANNEL

Heathy Hill

Droppy Nose
Point

Samson
Hill

Stony Porth

Rushy Bay

0   ½   1
KILOMETRES

0   ½   1
MILES

to be burial markers, while others may simply be the result of field clearance. In warmer Bronze Age times much of the land here was farmed. At first many of the cairns are not obvious to pick out against the surrounding rubble, but it is thought -provoking to realise that you may well be walking in a vast ancient burial ground.

Below Badplace Hill the earthworks form the landward defences of the Iron Age Cliff Castle which once provided a refuge against sea-borne raiders. The notorious nearby House of the Head, where Celtic tribesmen displayed their human trophies, probably acted as much as a deterrent against invaders as a place of worship.

Shipman Head Down offers a superb example of waved heath, with **Bell Heather, Ling** and **Western Gorse**. The scrub growing along the south side is made up of **European Gorse**. Just above the cliffs and coves an area of more species-rich grassland can be found. Here, **Thrift** mingles with **Yorkshire Fog, Buck's-horn Plantain, Spring Squill** and the nationally rare **Jointed Orange Bird's-foot** and **Hairy Bird's-foot Trefoil**. Other rarities such as **Golden Hair-lichen** and **Lungwort** add to the delight of visiting botanists.

Hell Bay

Hell Bay can more than live up to its name in bad weather. Then the furious cauldron of white water hurls itself at the cliffs below your feet and an impressive shudder can be felt through the rocks. Here the birdlife of Bryher can be seen against a spectacular backdrop. The cliffs here are home to summer colonies of **Herring Gull, Kittiwake, Razorbill** and **Shag**. **Ringed Plover** sometimes breed on the open heathland and **Kestrel** can occasionally be seen hovering above the cliffs.

Bird's-foot Trefoil

Heathy Hill and Rushy Bay

Both these sites lie at the southern end of Bryher. Heathy Hill is small – barely 10 metres high, and backed by sand dunes and grassland which cover a storm boulder beach. To appreciate the dune grassland here it is best to get down on your hands and knees; on Bryher, small really is beautiful. This is **Dwarf Pansy** territory. The species-rich grassland here also supports **Sand Sedge, Sea Stork's-bill, Buck's-horn Plantain, Thrift** and **Red Fescue**. Nationally scarce growths of **Sea** and **Portland Spurge** and **Western Clover** can be found. The low dunes are covered with **Marram** and **Sea Holly** along with **Sea Beet** around its edges. **Sea Kale** is more common down on the boulder-strewn strandline at the back of Stony Porth.

The top of Heathy Hill has an area of low-growing **Bell Heather, Ling** and **Western Gorse** with some rarer plants such as **Jointed Orange Bird's-foot, Autumn Lady's-tresses**, an exquisite little orchid, and **Small Adder's-tongue** fern. On the hillside the soil is deeper and dominated by **Bracken** although **Bramble** and **Honeysuckle** also grow. The coastal edge supports a good maritime grassland stretching out towards Droppy Nose Point. To the east of Rushy Bay the ground rises to give a grand view of the area from Samson Hill.

Great Pool and Little Pool

Great Pool is the only saline lagoon in Scilly, where the water is more salty than fresh. It is separated from the sea by a narrow storm beach known as Popplestone Bank. Although backed by a small system of sand dunes it was once regularly breached by storms. Imported granite now adds to the sea defence and is helping to protect the nearby houses and hotel. The pool supports several salt-tolerant plants in the water and around its margins. **Beaked Tasselweed** and **Sea-milkwort** grow thickly in the shallows, while the pool margin is fringed with **Saltmarsh Rush**. The pool also contains fish: **Grey Mullet** can sometimes be seen near the water's surface, and a nationally scarce **Sand Shrimp** can also be found.

The surrounding turf is made up of **Red Goosefoot** and **Lesser Sea-spurrey**. Beyond, the dunes are dominated by **Marram** with other maritime grassland plants including **Wild Carrot**. The nationally rare **Early Meadow-grass** also grows here.

Little Pool lies just to the north and is less brackish, which suits the growth of **Lesser Marshwort** and **Brackish Water-crowfoot** growing in open water. **Lesser Spearwort, Marsh Pennywort** and **Intermediate Water Starwort** prefer the margins.

Overleaf: Big seas in Hell Bay

Shag

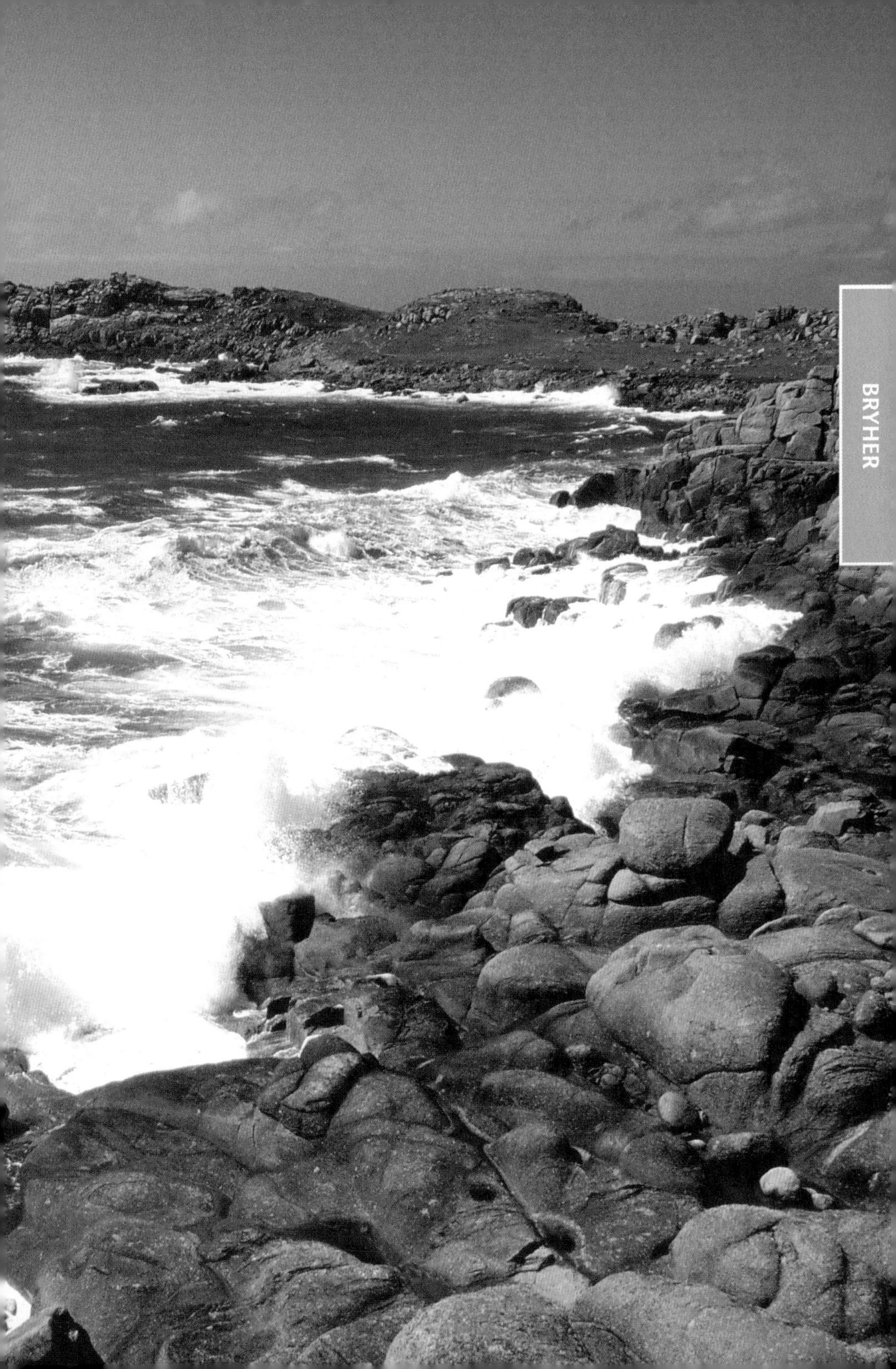

Samson

The magic of Samson, the largest uninhabited island in the archipelago, lures many visitors to its shores in summer. Lying just to the south of Bryher it is easily also recognised by its twin hills, which rise to nearly 30 metres in height. The hills are joined by a sand bar and occasionally the sea has been known to separate them during extremes of high tide and storm surges, but the wind soon restores the sandy ridge. Glorious views of the sunset over Samson and into the Atlantic Ocean beyond can be gained from The Garrison on St Mary's throughout midsummer. That view must have had the same attraction and perhaps some spiritual significance for ancient people, considering the number of hilltop tombs in Scilly.

Samson contains many interesting historical features, as well as a large seabird colony, and is easily reached by boat throughout the holiday season. The abundance of Bronze Age structures suggest Samson was once a more important place when Scilly was one large island. It was probably less than 500 years ago that the island finally split from Tresco and Bryher. Yet even today at low spring tide, it is still possible to wade just knee-deep across to Tresco.

In recent years Samson has perhaps become better known outside Scilly after the discovery of a famous wreck. *HMS Colossus* was returning home at the start of the winter of 1798, having played a significant part in Nelson's victory over Napoleon's navy at the Battle of the Nile. Damaged, and sheltering from a southerly storm, she lost her anchor and was driven aground. While the crew was saved, the ship was lost, along with priceless treasures of Greek and Etruscan pottery.

It is known that Samson was settled in 1669 after the Civil War. By the end of the eighteenth century there were six households and some thirty people resident, but the living the island offered could only be described as precarious. In 1855 the last three families were on the verge of starvation and were evacuated by Augustus Smith of Tresco. Since then the island has been left to the birds, rabbits and more seasonal visitors. Particular care must be taken not to disturb the large numbers of seabirds that nest throughout the summer months.

PLANT LIFE

The plant life of Samson is poor, with fewer than 130 species being listed, roughly half the number found on neighbouring Bryher. **Bracken** is the most obvious vegetation in summer, but a thriving colony of probably introduced **Primroses** can be seen near the remains of Amorel's Cottage. Here a **Tamarisk** and an **Elder** also grow. More commonly found is the **Bluebell**, which seems to thrive in quite a few places.

Grassland is now relatively scarce on the island as **Bracken** appears to have spread. However, **Ground Ivy, Balm-leaved Figwort** and **Woodsage** all seem to benefit from the cover provided by the Bracken foliage.

Heathland mainly covers the upper part of North Hill, while **Thrift** seems to do best around the low cliffs and **Marram** helps bind the sand. On the beach **Sea**

Sunset over Samson, from St Mary's

SAMSON

Rocket grows in profusion and its fragrance can fill the air. The **Small Bugloss** grows in sandy and waste places and may be locally common, so too is the **Biting Stonecrop**. **Pyramidal Orchids** have also been found.

More intriguing is a colony of the attractive blue-flowered **Greater Skullcap**, a member of the mint family that can be found at the southern tip. This plant grows nowhere else in Scilly and its appearance here is yet another island mystery.

BIRDS

Gulls are the biggest and noisiest birds on Samson. The nesting colony of **Lesser Black-backed Gulls** is one of the largest in Scilly, numbering over 1,000 pairs around South Hill. There is a cut path to the top of the hill, from where the private lives of these gregarious birds can easily be seen during May and June. However, be careful on approaching, as these gulls will sometimes dive-bomb intruders who get too close – so wear a hat! Early in the season is the best time, as the rapidly growing Bracken soon hides the youngsters when they begin to fledge. Large flocks of the adult gulls can sometimes be seen close inshore, especially in stormy weather, as they forage for food. They will rise into the air as a large wave breaks, then swoop down to seize anything brought to the surface by the turbulence. They winter further south on the Atlantic seaboard. It is interesting to note that the black colour of these Scillonian breeding gulls is not as dark as some of the autumn migrants that pass through from Scandinavia.

The **Great Black-backed Gull** is bigger. It also breeds on Samson, but not in such large numbers. Several pairs can, however, be seen on a small adjacent rocky outcrop off the west coast known as White Island.

Larger numbers of raucous **Herring Gulls** also nest on Samson closer to the beaches and all around the tops of the island's low cliffs.

Common Tern and even the rare **Roseate Tern** have been known to breed on the open heathland that covers North Hill but they are easily disturbed by thoughtless walkers. More often they may be seen on the neighbouring little Green Island off the southern shore, along with some **Sandwich Terns**.

Apart from **Tamarisk** and **Elder** shrubs, the total lack of trees means that **Bracken** provides the only real cover for more terrestrial birds. A few pairs of **Blackbird, Song Thrush** and a **Stonechat** or two may be seen, but many more **Wren** and **Rock Pipit** can commonly be seen along the shore. Occasionally a **Cuckoo** many parasitise a Pipit's nest and even **Ringed Plover** sometimes nest on the beach. More obvious is the **Oystercatcher**. A few seem to breed at the back of the beach every year during early summer.

Shelduck seem to have a tough time in Scilly. Some nest on Samson; deep down inside old rabbit burrows, where their eggs are safe from marauding gulls. The ducklings are not so lucky. They must leave to feed soon after hatching and so suffer heavy predation.

Autumn brings in many more birds. The sand flats are a good place to watch for waders. **Godwits, Grey Plover, Greenshank, Dunlin, Sanderling** and even **Curlew Sandpiper** may all forage off Samson at low tide. **Turnstones** can be seen year round and a few visiting ducks from nearby Tresco can also sometimes be found.

In winter, a few **Short-eared Owl** regularly hide amongst the Bracken, as do occasional **Woodcock**, especially in really cold weather.

MAMMALS

The **Scilly Shrew** can commonly be seen along the back of the island's beaches, foraging for **Sand Hoppers** amongst the stranded seaweed. Elsewhere their high-pitched shrieks can be heard amongst the bracken.

Rabbits once used to be very common on Samson, but myxomatosis seems to have killed them all at the same time as those on Bryher. Only on St Helen's, Tean and the Eastern Isles do populations appear to have escaped.

The largest mammal seen from Samson is the **Grey Seal**, but they are rarely seen ashore. Sometimes a seal can be watched hunting for fish off the rocks at the south end of the island.

Green Island and Stony Island

To the east of South Hill on Samson, these two islets are important bird breeding sanctuaries for **Common** and some **Sandwich Terns**. These delightful birds rarely nest in the south-west of England, and they cannot be found breeding anywhere else between Dorset and Wales.

Both of these little islets can be reached at low tide or by boat, and both have suffered in the past from disturbance by people. They are closed to visitors during the bird breeding season to prevent the carnage that can result from adult birds being driven off their nests. **Great Black-backed** and **Herring Gulls** are the most watchful predators in Scilly, so any eggs or nestlings left unguarded, even for a few minutes, are likely to end up as their lunch.

Gulls scavenging

Annet

The most important and probably best-known bird sanctuary in Scilly lies to the west of St Agnes. Annet is the largest of the Western Isles, a rugged little island open to the full force of the Atlantic. At just 18 metres high it is low-lying, and from the granite stack at the Haycocks to Annet Neck in the south, the rock is overlain by raised beach deposits. Prominent boulder-strewn storm beaches are a major feature, especially along its wave-battered western side.

SEABIRDS

Annet is of exceptional importance for its seabird breeding colonies. Eleven different species nest on the island, two of which, **Storm Petrel** and **Lesser Black-backed Gull**, are recognised as being of national importance. The island also supports the biggest colony of **Manx Shearwater** in Scilly. Not surprisingly access is carefully restricted and Annet is closed to visitors all year. Seabirds are most at risk to disturbance during their summer breeding season and in winter the island is an important place for adult and young seals to haul out.

Although home to the largest colony of **Puffin** in Scilly, they are greatly outnumbered by a more elusive seabird, the **Manx Shearwater**. This bird is a master flyer, best seen as it effortlessly rides the wind above the swell, skimming the waves with its long tapering wings. Hundreds are thought to nest deep in burrows on Annet. They only come ashore after dark, but can be best viewed on a balmy summer's evening when the sea becomes smooth and glassy. Large 'rafts' of shearwater gather to socialise at dusk before heading ashore to feed their young. Special boat trips are organised to watch the birds assembling in good weather.

Storm Petrels are much smaller, but although more numerous are far more difficult to see. By day they are either far out in the Atlantic or nesting deep underground amongst the boulders at the top of the shore. They too only come ashore after dark

Manx Shearwater   *Lesser Black-backed Gulls*
Overleaf: Manx Shearwater rafting between Annet and St Agnes

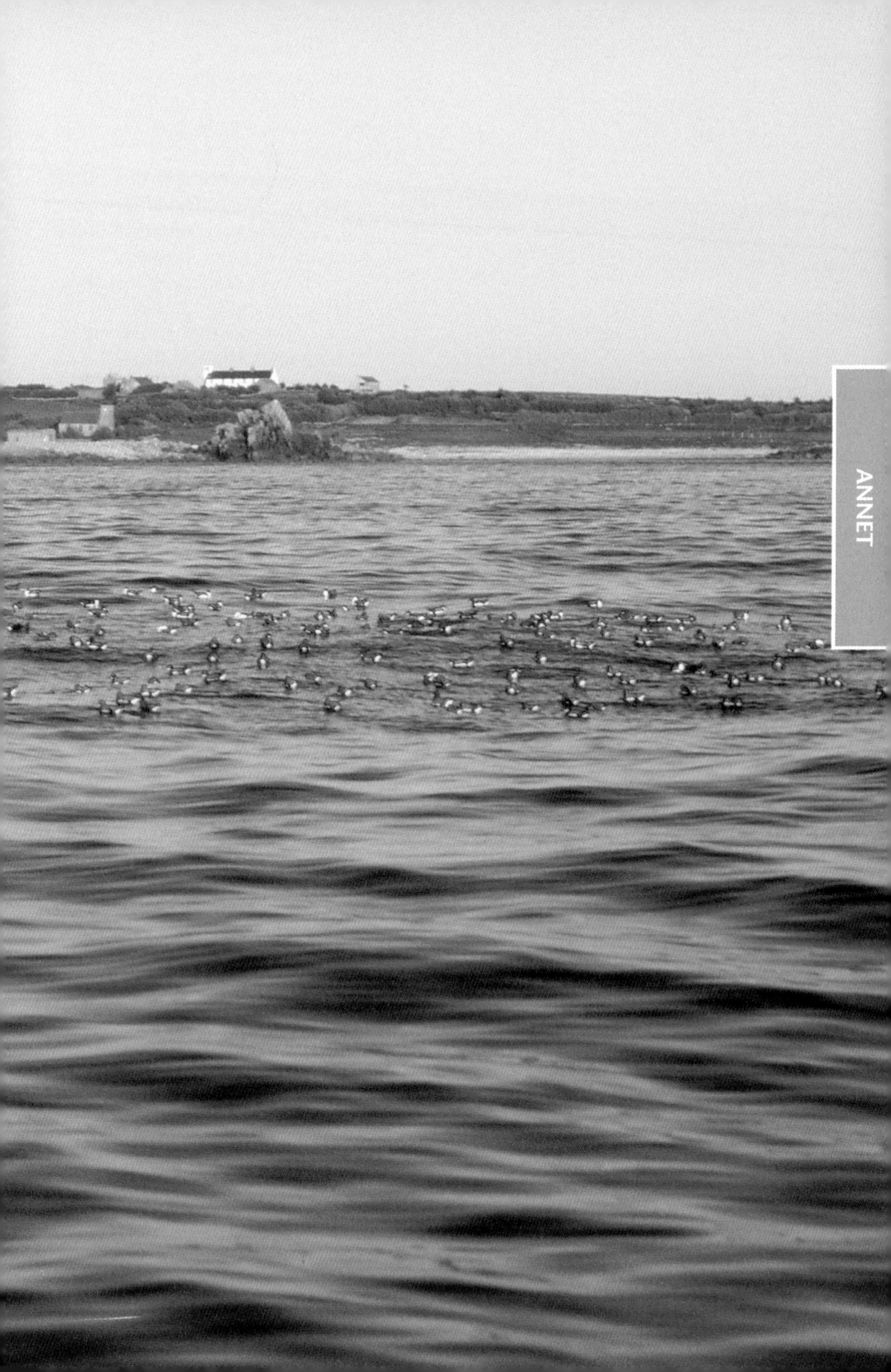

to nest and feed their young. They tend to breed in the older more stable beaches along the west and south side of the island.

The **Lesser Black-backed Gull** colony is mainly located amongst the **Bracken** and **Bluebell** areas south-east of Carn Windlass.

Puffin can best be seen by boat. Nesting in holes in the low cliffs on the eastern side, they can often be found not far away on the water or flying around before settling on a favoured rock. Other seabirds include **Herring Gull, Great Black-backed Gull, Fulmar, Razorbill, Common Tern, Kittiwake** and **Shag**.

PLANT LIFE

Annet is said to have the best-developed maritime heath anywhere in the British Isles. It is made up almost exclusively of **Thrift**, and is a sight to behold, especially in May when the multicoloured giant pink tufts are at their peak. Only 53 species of plants have been found on the island, and **Bracken** now dominates large areas. An invasion of **Yorkshire Fog** is thought to have occurred as a result of an accidental fire, but **Thrift** is now making a noticeable comeback. Other plants commonly found include **Bluebell** and **Lesser Celandine**, while the beaches support stands of **Tree Mallow** and **Sea Beet**. Annet can also claim two botanical rarities. In the south the nationally rare **Shore Dock** grows on the shingle beaches, and a nationally rare maritime lichen can be found on some of the granite outcrops.

Boulder beach on Annet   *Puffin*
Overleaf: Thrift on Annet

St Helen's

Little is known of the Celtic Christian saint St Elidius, whose name has been corrupted over time to St Helen. He is said to have been the son of a British king, and to have been a bishop in the early Christian church. The remains of a chapel and circular hermit cell on the island are thought to date from around the eighth century, yet it was another 300 years before a small church was built in his name. Some associated ruins were perhaps the homes of his followers. Apart from a brief use as a quarantine location for sick sailors in the eighteenth century, the island appears to have remained largely uninhabited since the fifteenth century. However, every year a service is still held on 6 August to celebrate the feast day of St Elidius.

PLANT LIFE

The island rises to over 40 metres and the lower slopes have deep soil covered by a tangle of **Bracken** and **Bramble**. This area also contains some rare **Balm-leaved Figwort** during summer. Access to parts of the island may be restricted during the bird breeding season. It is hoped that by limiting access more **Common Terns** may be tempted to nest as they have done in the past, particularly on the thin-soiled upper areas of heathland. Here the granite outcrops are festooned with lichen growth but elsewhere over the summit **Ling** and **Bell Heather** have colonised areas previously damaged by fire. In 1940 incendiary bombs set the island alight, and it was reputed to have burnt for days. Now, on the more open parts, **English Stonecrop** and **Buck's-horn Plantain** are the dominant plants. Large areas of the island have also become increasingly overrun by the fleshy leaves and exotic great flowers of the **Hottentot Fig**. Some large growths of **Mesembryanthemum** can also be found. Above the southern shore, where native **Small Reed** and **Tree Mallow** can be found, the maritime grassland supports good growths of **Thrift** and **Sea Beet**, as well as the nationally rare **Shore Dock**.

BIRDS

Only a scattering of **Herring Gull** and a few **Great Black-backed Gulls** nest on St Helen's, their nests of seaweed and exotic Mesembryanthemum or Fig usually being found perched on a granite outcrop or tucked into a cleft. An overflow colony of **Kittiwake** can also be found on the eastern cliffs, while a few **Puffin** may be seen on the west side looking out towards the main seabird breeding colony of Men-a-vaur.

St Helen's – Hottentot Fig flowers in the foreground with views over Tean towards St Martin's

Tean

Pronounced Tee-an, this delightfully sheltered little island consists of three small rocky hills. Great Hill is the largest, reaching over 40 metres in height. Between the granite outcrops lies deeper soil composed of glacial till and gravels. The beaches to the north and west of the island reveal the southern limit of glacial gravels that once spewed from great ice sheet to the north. Evidence of ancient human activity can also be found. Old walls lie between the little hills and the remains of a hut circle and more walling can even be found submerged in West and East Porth on the south side. There are also two entrance graves to be found, one on Great Hill and the other on the Old Man. Better known is ruin of an old chapel dedicated to St Theona, thought to have been a woman and perhaps living around the time of St Elidius.

PLANT LIFE

The summit of Great Hill supports some heathland but parts of Tean, which were perhaps once cultivated, are now covered in thick **Bramble** and **Bracken**. The island has a comparatively rich flora for its small size, partly due to its long habitation by people first in the Bronze Age, and then more recently from the late 1600s for over a century. Amazingly, a few pasture plants can still be found in the tiny fields: **Black Knapweed, Hop Trefoil, Red Clover, Rye Grass** and **Yellow Oat Grass** are all sur-vivors from an age of subsistence farming.

The dune grassland above East and West Porth is especially important for a tiny Scillonian speciality found nowhere else in Britain – the **Dwarf Pansy**. **Balm-leaved Figwort** and the rarer **Four-leaved Allseed** have both been discovered here. **Thrift** and **Sea Campion** grow abundantly in the maritime grasslands, and on the south side near to Clodgie Point, **Jointed Orange Bird's-foot** can be found.

BUTTERFLIES

The island is perhaps better known for its butterflies. The **Meadow Brown** seldom flies far and inbreeding can produce some interesting differences in the spot pattern on the wings. It is well known that different islands seem to have their own unique Meadow Browns, but Tean appears to have three distinct communities, one on each hill.

Another species was first described by a famous lepidopterist, E. B. Ford, in 1938. He thought it was a special island race, the **Tean Blue**. We now know from DNA investigation that it is a variety of the **Common Blue**; although paler in colour, it appears to be genetically no different from its nearby island relatives.

BIRDS

The island of Tean also has a small colony of **Puffin** on the eastern side, along with **Kittiwake, Lesser Black-backed Gull, Herring Gull** and some **Great Black-backed Gull**. In an attempt to improve the breeding success of the Puffin and perhaps even attract some nesting **Terns**, part of the island may be closed to visitors during their breeding season.

Round Island

Easily recognised by its conspicuous large lighthouse, Round Island can be seen from many parts of Scilly, and even from the cliffs of Land's End over 30 miles away. Built in 1887 and standing almost 70 metres above sea level, it is the most conspicuous marker in the islands. The island sits on the edge of the plateau that rises steeply from the surrounding sea bed. Storm-driven waves are reputed to rise suddenly and very high, occasionally throwing pebbles and seashells over the adjacent buildings.

Round Island is home to a pair of **Peregrine** and the summer residence of a large colony of **Stormy Petrel**. During the spring and autumn, especially in poor weather conditions, many small migrating birds are sometimes attracted by the light.

Round Island

Men-a-vaur

One of the most important seabird colonies in Scilly, Men-a-vaur is an impressive rock stack that rises sheer from the sea floor. Split into three giant granite slabs, huge waves can build spectacularly through the chasms to explode where they join. Almost impossible to land on except in the calmest weather, it is a place where only a few people have feared to tread. It is in any case closed to access during the bird breeding season.

Not surprisingly, its plantlife is rather limited, clinging to the bare rock face. There are, however, a few high shelves where **Tree Mallow** has taken precarious root, as well as **Orache** and **Common Scurvy Grass** grow.

Seabirds are Men-a-vaur's biggest claim to fame, with eight different species breeding here. The largest colony consists of **Razorbill** with some **Guillemot**. Good numbers of **Fulmar** and **Kittiwake**, and a few **Shag**, **Lesser Black-backed Gull**, **Great Black-backed Gull** and **Herring Gull** can all be seen during the breeding season.

Guillemot, including a Bridled form usually found further north

Overleaf: Men-a-vaur from St Helen's
Below: Men-a-vaur

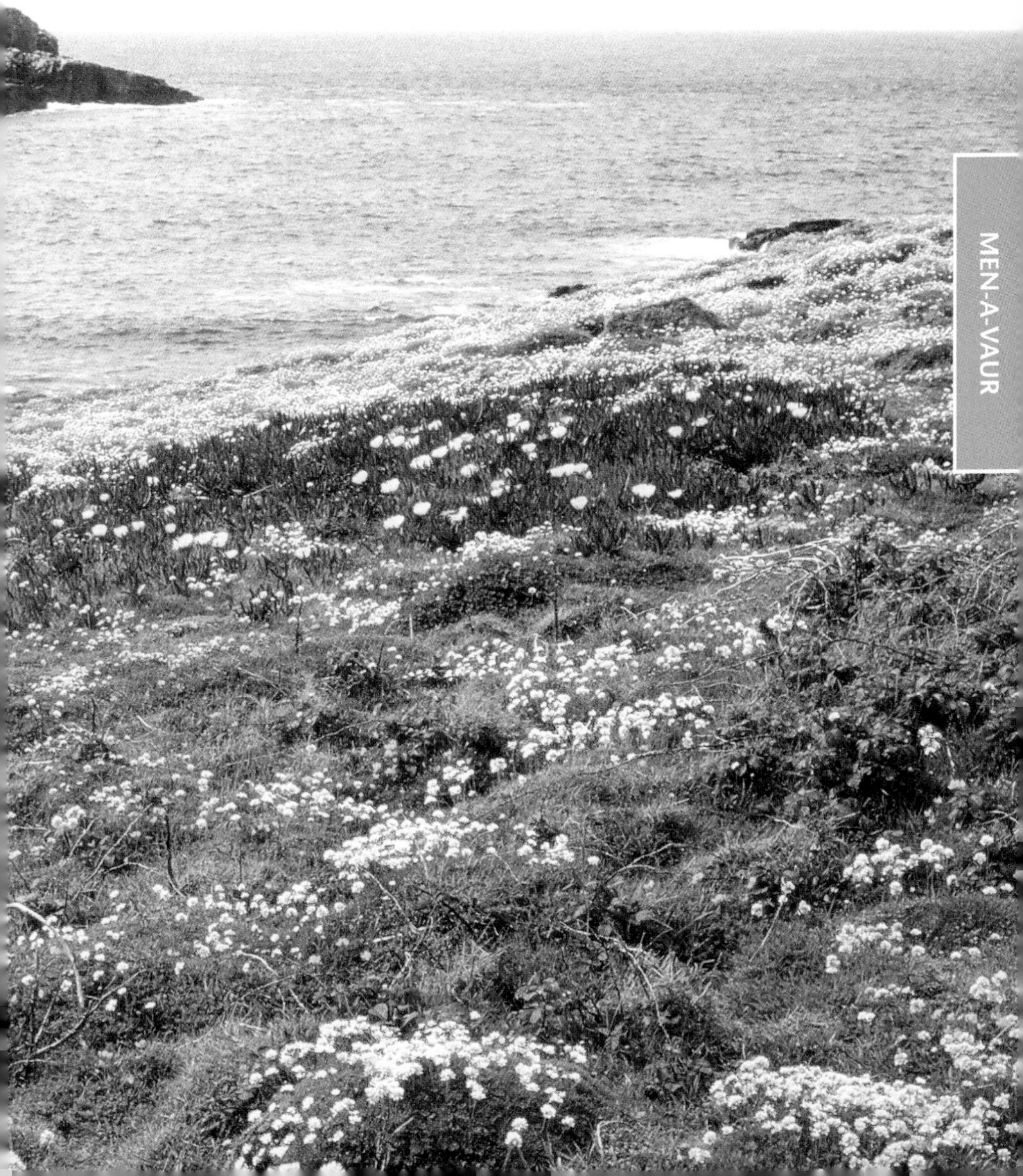

The Eastern Isles

A scattering of tantalising little islands nestle between the larger lands of St Mary's and St Martin's in the east of the archipelago. More magical and inviting than any others, the Eastern Isles are the first landfall for many people sailing into Scilly aboard *The Scillonian*. Many are little more than coarse granite peaks, others are green islands, and some are joined by fine white sandy or shingle bars. They include Great and Little Ganilly, Great, Middle and Little Arthur, Nornour, Great and Little Ganinick, Great and Little Innisvouls, Menawethan and the impressive Hanjague.

PLANT LIFE

Despite being sheltered from the worst of the south-western gales, their natural history is not rich. Even Great Ganilly, the largest of the group, only has 74 recorded plants out of 111 species found on all the Eastern Isles. The nationally rare **Jointed Orange Bird's-foot** grows on a small area of maritime heath on the northern side of the island. The lower coastal fringes are covered by maritime grassland where **Sea Beet** and **Thrift** commonly thrive; most of the steeper slopes are covered by a near-impenetrable mix of bracken and bramble.

Smaller areas of wind-blown sand between Great, Middle and Little Arthur support some good stands of **Marram**. **Sea Kale** commonly grows on the back shore between Great Ganilly and Nornour. The islands can also claim several more uncommon species, including **Sea Radish** and **White Ramping-fumitory**. **Shore Dock** and **Balm-leaved Figwort** are both nationally rare.

Even more remarkable, Great Ganilly is only other island in Scilly other than Tresco where **Oak** have been recorded as growing in recent times. The discovery of **Butcher's Broom** on the same island and on Nornour, has been attributed to the Roman settlement, shrine and evidence of trading which were discovered there. The settlement on Nomour, which was excavated in the late 1960s and early 70s, provided evidence of continual habitation from the late Bronze Age through to the Romano-British Iron Age. It is an amazing site. Some of the Romano-British buildings now lie partly submerged at high tide, a graphic reminder that the impact of global warming and rising sea levels is nothing new. Many of the artefacts found during the excavations of Nornour can be viewed at the fascinating little museum on St Mary's. Other finds of animal remains have provided good evidence of wildlife at that time.

BIRDS AND MAMMALS

The Eastern Isles support several large colonies of breeding seabirds during summer, mainly **Herring Gull**, **Great Black-backed Gull** and **Shag**. Smaller colonies of **Razorbill, Fulmar, Cormorant** and even a few **Puffin** can be seen during the early part of summer.

The one creature for which the Eastern Isles is perhaps most famed is the **Grey Seal**. An important colony of these impressive marine mammals can commonly be encountered basking on the rocks at low tide.

Grey seals basking in the Eastern Isles

Norrad Rocks

A scattering of small islands and formidably large rocks lie on the north-western edge of Scilly, partly protecting Bryher from south-westerly gales. These are the Norrad or Northern Rocks, and include Castle Bryher, Gweal, Illiswilgig, Maiden Bower, Mincarlo, Scilly Rock, and several other more isolated stacks and ledges. All are relatively low-lying, none exceeding more than 32 metres in height, but even that can seem daunting when approaching in a small boat.

Most of the rocks are difficult or almost impossible to land on, and in any case are closed to visitors all year round. The largest has a thin layer of soil and the others just a few deeper pockets. Exposed to salt spray and open to the wind, the plant life is limited to just six species of flowering plants. **Tree Mallow** is an uncommon shrub that tends to grow only where seabird guano enriches the soil. **Common Scurvy Grass, Orache, Rock Spurrey, Sea Beet** and **Thrift** are not so limited and will grow in surprisingly exposed maritime conditions. However, even some larger rocks such as Maiden Bower, support no flowering plants at all, owing to the frequency with which the sea washes entirely over them.

The only insect of note is an earwig – an island morph with exceptionally long pincers found also on the Western Rocks. However, the Norrad Rocks are very important for their breeding colonies of seabirds. Mincarlo has the largest breeding colony of **Cormorant** in the islands and a few **Puffin**, which also breed on Castle Bryher and Scilly Rock. Most of the larger rocks have **Shag** nesting on them along with **Fulmar, Razorbill, Herring Gull, Lesser and Great Black-backed Gulls. Storm Petrel** have only been reported from Mincarlo.

The rocks and ledges of the Norrad Rocks also contain some of the most important breeding grounds for **Grey Seal**.

Seal pup on Norrad Rocks

Western Rocks

The first landfall in the Western Approaches has a terrifying reputation as a mariner's nightmare. Lying to the west of the archipelago, the Western Rocks form a string of tiny islands stretching from Annet out to the Bishop Rock lighthouse. They include Hellweathers, Melledgan, Gorregan, Rosevean, Rosevear and Great Crebawethan.

Open to the full force of Atlantic gales these fearsome rocks, reefs and ledges are some of the most exposed islands off the British coast. So many wrecks have come to grief over the centuries that in some places they are stacked in the watery darkness, steel upon iron upon wooden hull. Hundreds of ships and thousands of poor souls perished here. Indeed this is where the Royal Navy suffered its greatest loss. In 1707 Admiral Sir Cloudsley Shovell was leading his squadron aboard his flagship, *HMS Association*, when they struck the Gilstone at night. Four ships went down within a few hours and some 2,000 sailors lost their lives. So disastrous was this navigational error that the Admiralty offered a prize for the most reliable way to calculate longitude.

Drifting today among the weather-smoothed granite on a rare morning of mid-summer calm is a surreal experience. The terrors of shipwreck seem a world away as the sea laps gently at the giant slabs and gurgles in the rock clefts. On the south-western side no weed clings to the granite. Not even barnacles can withstand the Atlantic pounding on the most exposed surfaces.

Bishop Rock lies four miles beyond the inhabited islands, with reputedly the most exposed lighthouse in the British Isles. The tower is perched on a granite pinnacle barely 46 by 16 metres wide that rises over 45 metres from the seabed. The rock itself is almost completely covered at high spring tide and reveals no white water to warn of the reef below which is a major hazard for shipping.

PLANT LIFE

Even the largest of the Western Rocks is only 17 metres high, and they are saturated with salt spray for much of the year. Soil is rare in such places and usually thin and poor. Elsewhere only pockets survive the winter gales. Conditions here are so bad that only six species of flowering plants have been found. All grow on Rosevear, the largest island in the group and the only one to have offered a summer residence to workmen. The Blacksmith's Shop, now a ruin, was built during the construction of the Bishop Rock lighthouse. Only **Tree Mallow** grow in any abundance, thriving wherever guano enriches the soil. **Common Scurvy Grass**, **Curled Dock**, **Orache**, **Rock Spurrey** and **Sea Beet** can also be found.

BIRDS

The Western Rocks are far richer in bird life with eleven species of breeding seabirds. **Great and Lesser Black-backed Gulls**, **Herring Gull**, **Fulmar** and **Puffin** all nest here. Some islands seem to be favoured by certain birds. The population of **Shag** in Scilly is of national importance, and the biggest numbers nest on Rosevear. In contrast Gorregan is better known for its **Kittiwake** colony, along with **Guillemot** and **Razorbill**. Cormorant breed on Melledgan and **Storm Petrel** have been discovered nesting in some of the boulder beaches.

Rosevear with old blacksmith's shop

MAMMALS

Inaccessible and remote, these islands are the most important breeding grounds in Scilly for the **Grey Seal**. At low water they can be seen basking on the rocks. Their favoured haul-outs include Little Crebawethan, Wee Rock and Grear. At high tide they are off fishing but can still be seen bobbing about in the surf, seemingly dangerously close to the rocks.

Where to Find Wildlife

Where to find wildlife

The secret to discovering nature is – time and place. If you know the right place to go, at the right time, your chances of finding wildlife is greatly increased. Different animals and plants like to live in different conditions. Some like it wet, others dry. Some like acid soil, others alkaline which is rich in calcium. Each of these habitats will have its own communities of wild animals and plants. The Isles of Scilly are one of the best places to clearly see these different habitats, often side by side separated by just a short walk.

Introduction to Scilly habitats

Stroll along any of the islands' shores lapped by gentle waves. Fine white sand squeezes between your toes before being washed away in the sparkling clear sea. Turning inland you pass through a narrow band of salt-tolerant plants growing above the strand line, before scrambling up and over tall grass-topped dunes. Heading inland through rich maritime grassland and up onto higher ground, you are treading among waved heathland in a primeval landscape. In other places, the sheltered coastal fringe gives way to freshwater wetlands with pools, marsh and swampland. Elsewhere along the outer edge of the islands, the shore is more exposed. Here, rock ledges and boulder-strewn beaches back onto low sea cliff, topped by maritime heath with pink tufts of Thrift.

In all these places many wild plants and animals survive. Yet of all the creatures in Scilly none is more obvious than the birds. The uninhabited islands are home to internationally important colonies of breeding seabirds, and non-breeding shore birds. It seems they have everything they need: undisturbed islets for nesting, plenty of food in the species-rich sand flats and rocky shores, wave-tossed open sea, as well as quiet places to roost at high tide.

The Isles of Scilly contain thirteen officially recognised different habitats. Additionally the gardens of Scilly are also special places with their own wild communities. There are few other places in Britain where the natural succession of habitats from seashore to hilltop can so clearly be seen.

Farmland

Several hundred acres of land are cultivated in Scilly and many of the wild plants found here are very special. Some can be found on the mainland but others grow here in far greater numbers, while a few are very special to Scilly. The communities of these wild weeds seem to vary not only between islands but also from field to field.

Spring comes early to Scilly, and the cultivated Narcissi and Daffodils can be well

Escallonia flowering on Tresco

into bloom before Christmas and then die down in early spring. But it is not long before the fields glow again with renewed colour, but this time they are weeds.

Sadly, modern farming methods and more efficient herbicides have reduced the number of rare species on some farms, while other previously cultivated fields have been left to revert to rank growth unsuitable for arable weeds. However, the sight that brightens the stay of so many holiday visitors can still regularly be seen – fields of flowers. **Look out for colourful arable weeds and Song Thrush**.

Shelterbelts and Hedgerows

Protection from the wind and salt spray is vital to produce any crop in the islands, so an effective system of shelterbelt trees and hedgerows was developed by trial and error. The combination of trees, low walls of stone and taller growths of evergreen shrubs provide the required filtering effect. The resulting tiny fields contain a micro climate all of their own. In Scilly small is beautiful for wild flowers.

The island's hedgebanks are probably unique in Britain for their healthy stands of Elm trees, whereas on the mainland, Dutch Elm disease continues to ravage any surviving English elms. In Scilly, trees are a vital first line of defence against Atlantic gales and sea breezes, while the best hedgerows tend to have dense, shrubby growth. The most effective species are exotic, and commonly planted ones include the Monterey Pine and hedge-forming shrubs such as Euonymus, Pittosporum, Escallonia, Oleria, Hebe and even Tamarisk. All seem salt-tolerant to some degree. **In summer, introduced Escallonia hedges come into full bloom, although it may be seen flowering in other seasons too.**

Freshwater

Pure freshwater is very precious on any small island surrounded by sea. Salt spray can travel far inland when driven by Atlantic gales so any freshwater pools can become contaminated from time to time.

Giant Echium in Abbey Gardens   *Waved heath on Bryher*

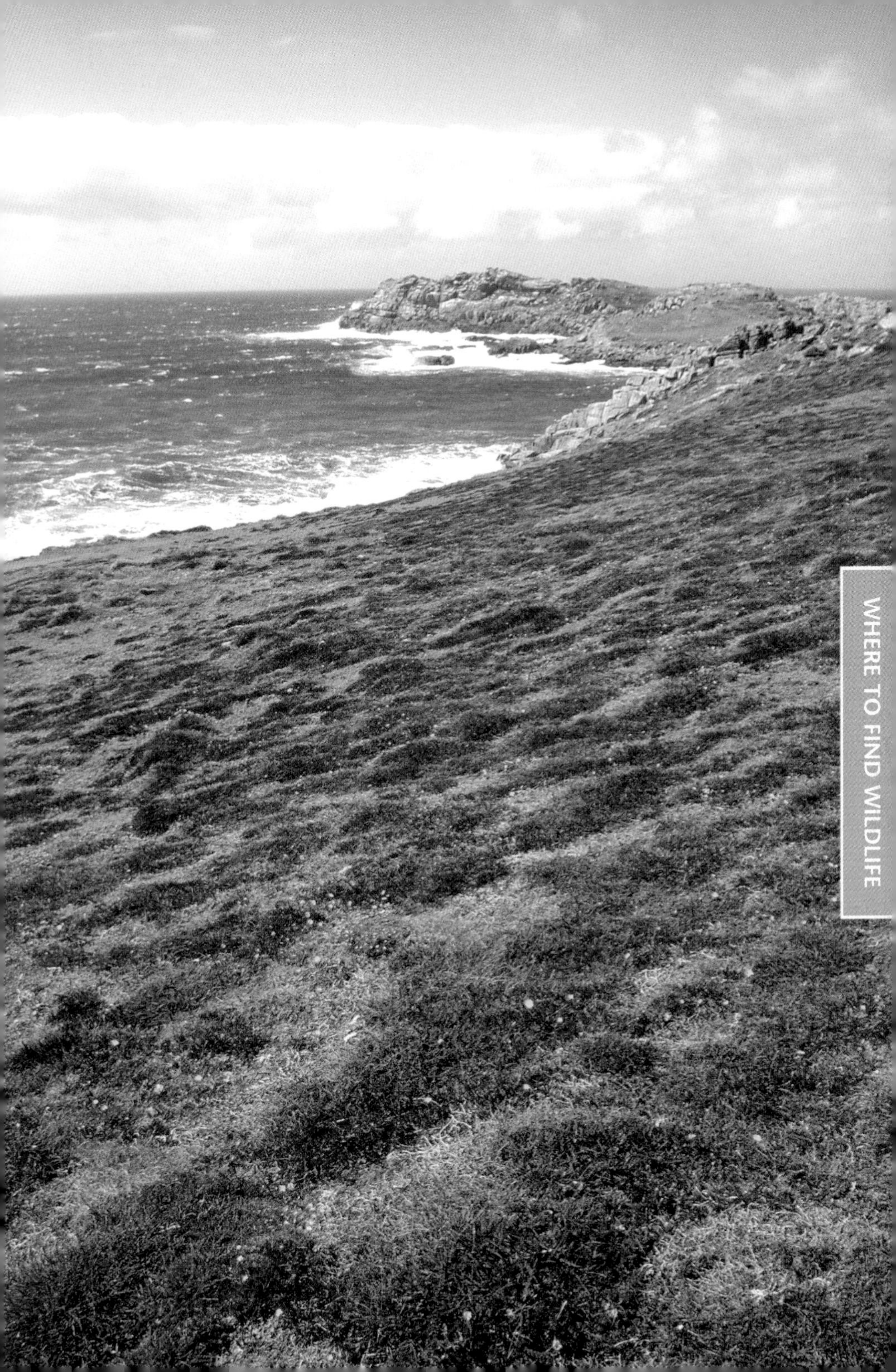

There are just three main freshwater wetlands in Scilly: Great Pool on Tresco, and Higher and Lower Moors on St Mary's. All are valuable as feeding grounds for migrating and wintering birds, as well as breeding sites for waterfowl and summer visitors, such as warblers. Great Pool on Tresco is always worth a visit, particularly in spring and autumn when migrant wildfowl, waders and even rare grebe may be seen. **Look out for huge Tussock Sedges, birds bathing and warblers amongst the reeds.**

Gardens

Towering palms, colourful tropical plants and nectar-sipping birds – surely this cannot be part of England! Many exotic plants thrive in the largely frost-free climate of Scilly. Throughout the summer, colourful blooms and outlandish foliage drape over walls or burst from garden gates. The larger inhabited islands have surprisingly exotic gardens protected by tall hedges, but none comes close to the scale and stature of the Abbey Gardens on Tresco, originally laid out by Augustus Smith in 1834. **Watch for nectar-sipping birds throughout the warmest months.**

Maritime Heathland

To travel back in time and see some original prehistoric vegetation, walk along any of the island's coastal fringes exposed to the harshest winds. Here the soil is thin and acidic, swept by salt-laden spray. Yet plants and animals live here that seem to revel in such terrible conditions. These areas of maritime heathland and grassland are especially important for rare oceanic lichens, and also as breeding grounds for many of the islands' seabirds. At its most severe, where wind-blasting lays the plants low and stems bare, Heather is the dominant plant. Growing away from the prevailing breeze they only flower in the lee. The effect of the wind on the plant growth creates a series of living ridges, a rolling sea of Heather better known as 'Waved Heath'. This rare primeval landscape also bears more than a passing resemblance to those found much further south on the western seaboard of Europe. Plants rarely found, or absent elsewhere in Britain, seem to flourish here, forming an intriguing, so-called 'Lusitanian' flora.

Heathland, sometimes referred to in Scilly as 'Down', also contains more sheltered, sandy parts and these are some of the best areas to find beetles, butterflies and bees. In undisturbed parts and on remote islands, heathland is also important for breeding seabirds, especially gulls as well as Tern, Puffin and Manx Shearwater. **The heather first begins to appear in July and can often last well into August and early September.**

Saline Lagoons

Saline pools typically contain a mix of fresh and salty water. Open areas of freshwater that collect close to the sea are vulnerable to salt-water inundation. Seawater

Tresco Abbey Gardens

either percolates slowly through shingle ridges or can be dumped by big seas surging up and over a beach, or through a connecting drainage channel.

Bryher boasts the only true saline lagoon in Scilly, known as the Great Pool, but on St Agnes, Big Pool and the adjacent Little Pool – the only areas of open water on the island – are separated from the sea by a narrow and sometimes mobile shingle and boulder beach, and the sea occasionally tops the bank during severe winter storms. For much of the year, however, the pools on St Agnes are usually more fresh than salty, although evaporation of the water in the heat of summer can increase its salinity. Large numbers of gulls can often be seen bathing in these lagoons.

Sand Dunes

Daybreak on any beach in Scilly is special. The piping calls of Oystercatcher and the cry of gulls greet the summer dawn. Sunrise casts shadows over the sandy shore, and the warmth of a new day is tempered by the coolness of crystal-clear water swirling around one's feet. Sinking into the white softness, footprints leave a temporary trail until the turn of the tide. Fine sand is the essential ingredient for a good beach, and in Scilly it is not in short supply. The mixture of shell fragments and finely ground grains of rock have a quality quite different from other beaches even nearby. Although carried by the same currents and deposited by waves, sand has a composition and character unique to every shore. While the fragmented remains of millions of seashells make up part of it, the finest white sand in Scilly is the result of gigantic glaciers pulverising granite in the dim and distant past. **The dunes of Scilly can look especially exotic in summer when the introduced blue Agapanthus flowers.**

DUNE FORMATION

Underwater, the sand may have travelled many miles, and that movement is continued onshore by the breeze. As the tide ebbs from the beach, more sand is exposed. Sun and wind rapidly dry the surface layers. Gusts then gather the finest grains, driving them into great piles. A dune is born. The tallest dunes can eventually reach over 30 metres high, yet strong winds will continue to move them. The process is intriguing to watch. It occurs wherever there is fine sand, from the driest tropical deserts to the shores of Scilly. Sand particles blown up the gentle windward slope pour over its crest. Then, in a series of miniature landslips it slides down a steeper face. Blasted and battered by gales with new supplies of sand reinforcing the front, ranks of dunes advance slowly inland. In this way dunes move relentlessly forward.

Dune formation seems to have accelerated during historical time. The discovery of old buildings on the Cornish mainland inundated by sand provide proof of their massive movement.

Most of the larger islands have some dunes and grassland, but Tresco has some of the biggest and best developed. Other areas include Bar Point on St Mary's and Higher Town and Great Bay on St Martin's.

When sand is on the move it seems as if nothing on earth can stop it, but plants can – almost. By trapping and binding the grains they can at least slow the move-

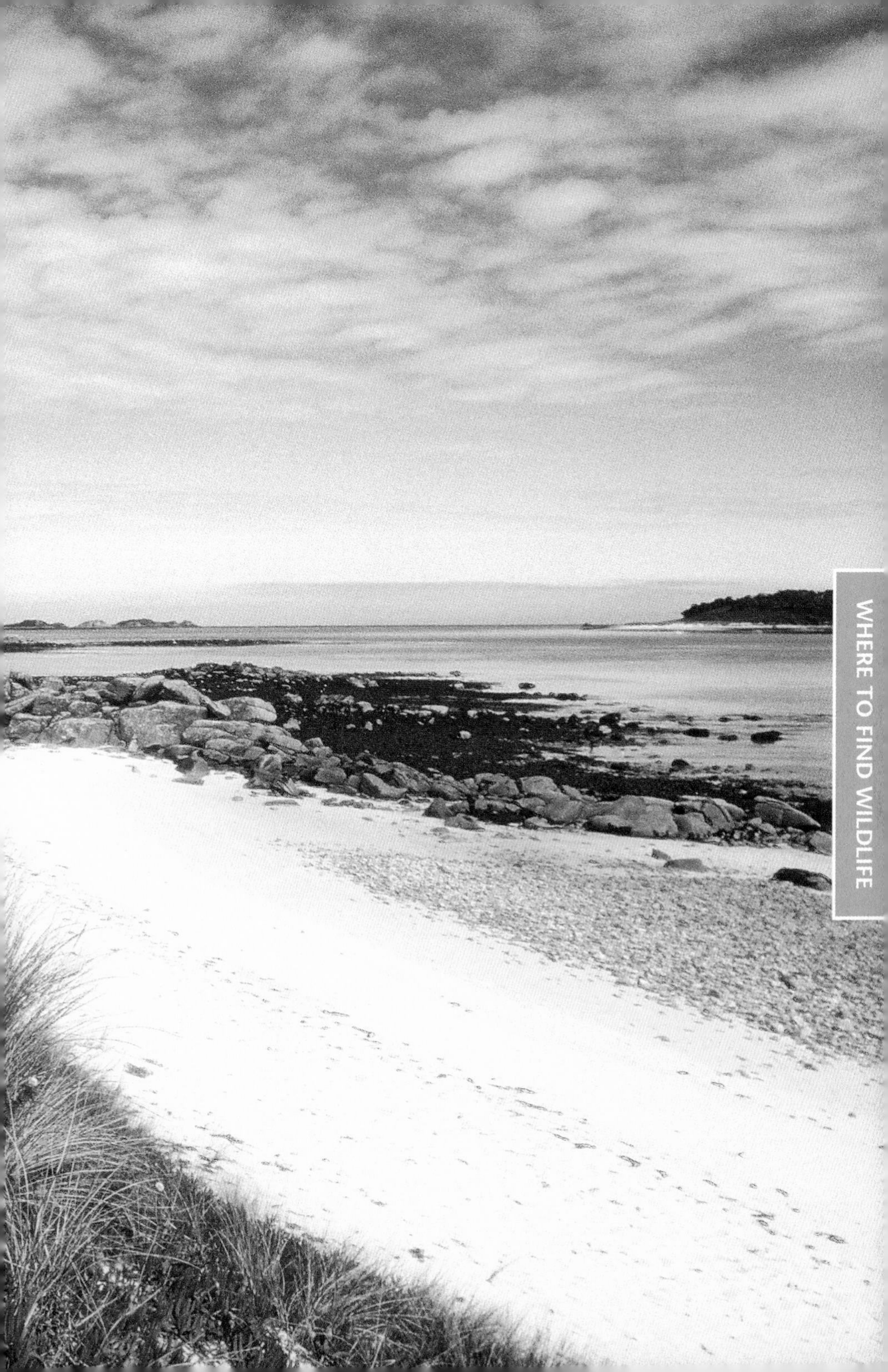

ment to a trickle. The process of consolidation begins first down on the shore. Where waves deposit a strandline of rotting seaweed, nutrients leach into the sand. Few plants can survive the harshness of the conditions here between land and sea. There is no soil or humus and the only minerals come from the remains of shells. At high noon on a cloudless day the sun bakes the beach. Temperatures can soar to 60°C, while at night they plummet. Drying winds bring more salt-laden sand and the returning tide threatens to drown the top of the shore. So only during summer when this area is beyond the tide's reach, can a few special plants take root. Marram is the best builder of dunes. As sand is trapped between its growing stems and roots, it slows the processes of wind erosion and the dunes grow taller.

The flora of sand dunes is particularly well studied. Dunes can be unstable enough at the best of times and much movement has already taken place over many years. But not all is natural. Some sand movement is caused by human disturbance. Today the biggest threat to dunes comes from people – trampling, lighting fires, litter, vehicles, and even taking sand for building. For all their enormous scale, sand dunes are incredibly fragile. If the protecting plants are destroyed they can easily be blown away.

DUNE SYSTEMS

Marram also helps other less tolerant plants to survive by consolidating the first line of sand mountains – the so-called younger yellow dunes. These seldom exceed more than 15 metres and are often very mobile. Yellow dune has no soil, and Marram is the dominant growth, but between its growth some Sea Holly, Sea Spurge, Red Fescue grass, Sand Sedge and Cat's-ear may also be found.

Beyond the yellow dunes is a small valley, known as the dune slack. The next line of dunes can grow bigger but seldom reach any great height in Scilly. Even these mountains can sometimes move in storm-force winds. But beyond them, through the fine wind-jostled leaves of Marram is a sheltered, older dune slack, often with some permanent pools of water, known locally as pans. These can support a more interesting community of plants and animals. The water is often a rich reddish-brown in colour, as a result of an oxide of iron. Rainfall here is not high, but at night even in summer, temperatures can plummet. The heavy dew that results helps plants survive the driest months.

The next ridge of so-called fixed dune is lower and relatively static. Further inland a scattering of sand hills can then merge into sandy pasture. These older dunes are known as Grey dunes.

Sea Cliffs

Few experiences rival the fascination and fear of standing on a cliff edge in the teeth of a howling Atlantic gale. The taste of salt on your lips, wind tearing at your clothes and the scream in your ears is like nothing else on earth. Far out in the Atlantic Ocean a storm is racing towards the Western Approaches. The sea swell produced by the depression arrives ahead of the rain, rolling relentlessly towards the land. Rank upon rank of huge waves rear their heads before toppling forward as their tops tear open,

Tresco channel and Bryher beyond

revealing a wall of white water hurling itself at the cliff face. The tremor from each gigantic explosion sends a judder through your body as the energy of over 1,000 miles is unleashed at your feet.

The history of the earth's formation is held within its rocks. There are few places where these can be more clearly read than in the sheer face of a coastal cliff. No matter whether the rock originally came from the fiery furnaces of past volcanic activity, ancient reefs or deposits of glacier-borne silt many millennia ago, they now lie exposed and are gradually being worn away. The destructive energy of wind and wave can be felt as well as seen, and cliffs have other forces at work on them that, although more subtle, can move mountains bit by bit.

Most rocks acquire fractures and faults as a result of titanic pressures and strains. Winter rain seeping into these cracks can freeze overnight and expand. The resulting forces shatter the surface, prise off slabs of rock and turn hairline cracks into yawning fissures. Year after year the relentless cycle of freezing and thawing eats into the coast. At the foot of the cliff, the action of waves scours away softer rocks and gnaws away at its base. The resulting overhang eventually becomes unstable and falls into the waves. Slowly but surely the sea gains at the expense of the land.

The sea cliffs of Scilly are generally low. Composed of hard granite, few are more than 30 metres high and most are much lower. In the most exposed places their granite is worn smooth by the action of wind and sea over immense periods of time. All the island cliffs offer breathtaking scenery, sumptuous sea views and a veritable feast of wild flowers. Nesting seabirds add another dimension, filling the invigoratingly pure air with their summer cries. As a vantage point for watching nesting behaviour, aerial antics and migratory movements, cliff tops are unsurpassed.

Look out for Kittiwakes and Fulmar nesting on low cliffs. They are especially approachable in Scilly but be careful not to disturb them when they have eggs or young as Herring Gulls will rob their nests.

Low tide reveals granite boulders, old walls and sand flats
Tresco: New Grimbsy harbour entrance with Cromwell Castle

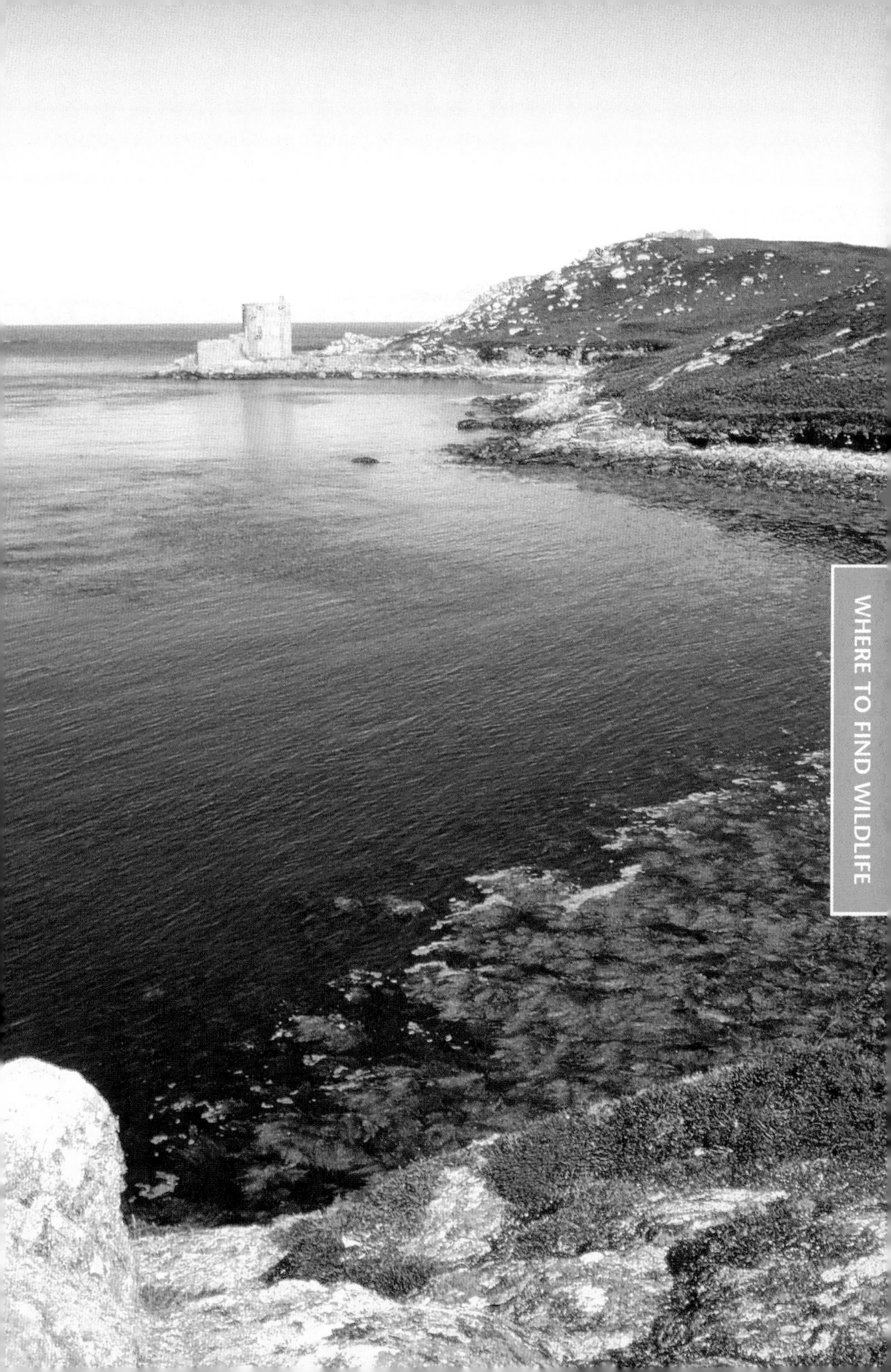

Sea and Shore

The shores of Scilly are amazing. Sparkling clear water, rich marine life and an abundance of shipwrecks give the islands an enviable reputation for some of the best diving, snorkelling and beachcombing in Britain. Many areas are of national and some of international importance. They include Boulder Beaches, Rocky Shores, Sandy Shores and Mud Flats, Subtidal Rocks, Eel Grass Beds and the Open Sea.

On the exposed outer edges the shores consist mainly of bare rock and storm-driven boulder beaches. These are fearful places in a gale, when waves that have travelled 1,000 miles or more unleash their energy in a few spine-tingling seconds. Yet on the most sheltered inner shores peace and tranquillity reign, especially during the warmest months. Rock pools are full of weird and wonderful life; beneath the mirror smooth surface, trapped by the outgoing tide, is a fantastic collection of marine creatures. Here prawns prance, crabs creep and squat lobsters skulk. Rock pooling must surely be one of the simplest and most satisfying pleasures for children and big kids alike. But what makes our seashore so rich?

The vast expanse of the Atlantic Ocean bathes British shores in its relentless eastward drift and warm prevailing winds. The ocean movement owes its origin mainly to the mighty Gulf Stream which starts in the Caribbean Sea. Here its boundless warm flow, around 100 kilometres wide and reaching a kilometre deep is driven by the rotation of the earth and unfailing south-westerly winds. Crossing the ocean into the colder waters of the western Atlantic, it spreads into four currents, and slows. Turbulence brings up nutrients from the sea floor to feed a rich supply of microscopic marine life. By now it is more accurately known as the North Atlantic Drift and the Isles of Scilly lie directly in its path. While the main flow passes up the west coast towards Scotland, another enters the English Channel. And so it is the Gulf Stream that gives rise to the incredible fertility of the seas around the Isles of Scilly.

Central to the islands are the shallows separating St Mary's, St Martin's, Tresco, Bryher and Samson. In places it is possible to walk between many of the isles at low spring tide. Wade in the lee of an island on a

Topshells on strand line   *Rocks showing seaweed zones*

warm day and you are in another world. Here the biggest waves are ripples made by your own splashing feet. The ebb of the crystal-clear water at low tide reveals a fascinating yet curiously strange shore. Many common mainland species are absent or rare while others not normally found in Britain are abundant. It is a pattern repeated at all levels, both on land and at sea. In the coarser gravels giant topshells, tube-dwelling parchment worms and a burrowing anemone are notable rarities. There are also four types of seaweed, more accurately known as marine algae, which are of national importance. In all some 128 different seaweeds, 13 lichens and 237 animals have so far been recorded from these shores.

The sea around Scilly is very clear. The absence of rivers transporting mud or industrial effluents gives the water a clarity that draws scuba divers from around the world. Now the entire offshore area has been declared a marine park and is protected down to the 50-metre contour. This remarkable environment encompasses a seascape of great extremes, from gentle flats where the sand is so fine and waters so calm that beds of Eel Grass can grow, to the incredibly rugged Western Rocks. When a marine survey of Britain was undertaken a new shore type was added especially for the Isles of Scilly. To describe the extremes of underwater chasms and sheer walls, sharp reefs and wave-smashed ledges of the Western Rocks, a new category of 'super-exposed' was added. It is amazing how living organisms survive such appalling conditions, yet they do – and thrive. In deeper water, colourful, long-lived and slow-growing sea fans and corals cling extravagantly to the rocks.

Seashores can broadly be divided into two types, each with their own characteristic communities of wildlife.

ROCKY SHORES

Twice daily a vast area of seabed is exposed to the air and twice it is drowned. Unlike a sandy shore, where animals can burrow for safety, on rock there is often no place to hide. Captured in countless rock pools at low tide, thousands of creatures must survive the rigours of the elements and predators until the sea returns. Life in a pool is no picnic. Sunlight is essential for seaweed growth but heat the marine creatures can do without. Warm water can reduce the levels of life-giving oxygen as well as threatening to cook the inhabitants. Rain dilutes its salinity. Gulls will feed on anything they can reach. In summer other scavengers arrive, often hunting in packs. A combination of curiosity and excitement brings an army of groping fingers and sweeping nets. The harvest is a haul of hapless creatures plucked from their temporary homes and placed in plastic buckets. Even among young children the hunting instinct is strong. But creatures replaced within a few minutes generally survive unharmed. If upturned stones are also put back the urge is satisfied and life in the pool can continue undisturbed, at least until the next ebb tide.

Rocky shores are rich foraging grounds, and not just for children. Different rocks weather and erode at different rates and in different ways, so some shores have better rock pools than others. However, the life of shores is more heavily influenced by their exposure to wind and wave than pure geology. In terms of their wildlife they can broadly be divided into exposed, semi-exposed and sheltered shores.

Exposed shores are open to the full force of the Atlantic, hammered by exploding waves and scoured by strong currents. This applies to most of the outer shores,

LIchen-covered rocks are a feature of Scilly

especially those facing south-west, and headlands take a real battering. Only a special sort of life can survive here, like the Limpet that lives in its own bomb shelter.

Semi-exposed shores suffer less violent conditions, often protected by headlands or rocky islets offshore and are usually dominated by forests of wrack – brown seaweeds. Sheltered shores are mainly found along the inner coast and in the most sheltered coves.

The life of a rocky shore is not randomly scattered. The highest part has the most limited marine life because it is exposed to the air for longest. Here life must also withstand being heated by the sun and drenched in freshwater when it rains. Further down the shore these hazards become less of a problem. The result is that different parts, from top to bottom are dominated by different forms of life best able to cope with the conditions. The banding this produces can sometimes be quite striking. So the life of a rocky shore between high and low water marks can be broadly divided into zones – the upper, middle and lower shore. On a shallow, sloping site these zones may be wide, while on a steep face they will be narrow.

Sea spray can affect the growth of other plants on rocky shores way above the level of the highest tides. But marine plant life is special. Although the pounding of waves can be severe, the sea is relatively warm. Light is gradually filtered as it passes through water, so most weed growth occurs in shallow seas. In the clear water around Scilly it may reach 50 metres of usable light apart from when algal blooms reduce transparency to the level of pea soup. Conditions are very different from dry land. At low tide swathes of seaweed hang limp. Dry on top, they remain moist underneath, covering the rocks in a slippery shaggy rug. As the sea returns they are transformed. Their drab fronds lift and sway with the waves.

But in the sea the biggest problem is staying put. The holdfast of algal weeds has no other function than to grasp rock. Water can support the plant, so a rigid stem is not necessary if fronds can float. But the plant must be strong enough to withstand the battering action of waves and exposure to fresh air. Around 700 different types of marine algae live on British shores. Some are more dominant than others and it is these seaweeds along with the animal life, that best distinguish the different zones.

Above all else is the splash zone. Here few plants can survive, yet colourful orange and grey lichens seem to thrive. Lichens are extraordinary. They are made up of two different plants living together – an alga and a fungus. Both gain from the relationship, surviving in places where each would perish alone. Below the splash zone lies a band of black lichen right on the high water line, where they are only briefly immersed in the sea.

Beyond the lower shore lies the Laminaria zone, deeper water, seldom ever exposed by even the lowest spring tide. This is where the kelp beds begin. Kelp or Laminaria as it is more properly known, is a tough plant. It needs to be – wave action here can be powerful. Light levels are low and competition for space is intense as conditions are less stressful than further up the shore. Marine animal life is also abundant in the Laminaria zone. In sheltered shallows the Little Egret, an exotic-looking pure white bird, adds a touch of glamour to Scillonian shores.

SANDY SHORES

Scilly has some of the finest sandy beaches to be found, some shingle and a few more pebbly in nature. But the most enchanting are the so-called shell beaches. Many sandy coves have parts where different sea shells seem to accumulate. But just occasionally, where wind and tides combine in some extraordinary way, vast quantities of exquisitely formed empty mollusc homes can be washed ashore. The yellow periwinkles are the most conspicuous. They tend to be found in the most sheltered waters, while darker ones live on more exposed shores. The Tiny Cowrie shell is one of the rarest and most beautiful to find. Locally known as 'guinea moneys', they can most frequently be found on Tresco's southern shore.

Onshore every tide brings a potential harvest for the beachcomber. Strandlines fascinate people and provide a twice daily food delivery service for scavenging birds. Several days of strong prevailing winds from the west usually bring the best haul. Then the tides can leave real evidence of the Gulf Stream's exotic origins. The seeds of tropical trees, big Macuna and Entada beans from the Caribbean and South America are not uncommon treasures.

Neptune Grass is only found growing in the Mediterranean and as far north as the Bay of Biscay. While it does not grow in Scilly its leaves often turn up on the shore as small balls not much bigger than a little fingernail. Rolled about by the waves, Neptune leaves and sand form what are commonly called sea-balls.

The remains of fish, egg cases, and crabs litter the strandline, but by far the most common flotsam is seaweed. If you disturb a piece of weed then a hopping hoard of tiny creatures leaps into action – Sand Hoppers. Related to shrimps they appear to be curled up and compressed sideways – a shape which may help them burrow in the sand. The power of their jump is impressive, sometimes over two metres. They are scavengers, feeding on the decaying life of the strandline and can occur in large numbers. Up to 25,000 have been counted on a single square metre of sand. Along with kelp flies, they can be more of a nuisance than a menace. But after dark they do seem attracted to light. Beach barbeques glowing strongly at night seem particularly inviting to these nocturnal hoppers.

Keep an eye open for exotic seeds and shells as well as bits of blue and white china washed ashore from a wreck, or small flint scrapers last used by a Bronze Age fisherman.

Strandline – Tresco with sea kale at top of beach

PLANTS AND ANIMALS

Plants

A thin layer of acid soil mixed with sand covers much of the island's granite. In such poor turf only Heather, Ling and other heathland plants can thrive. Elsewhere deeper soils have formed from glacial deposits on St Martin's and the northern isles, and the rubble remains of decomposed granite that have created head deposits on the larger islands and some of the smaller ones. Here deeper-rooted plants can grow. The usually mild climate enables many plants to grow in sheltered places throughout the year, so Scilly supports a surprisingly large variety of plants, some of which can be found nowhere else in Britain. Rainfall is adequate and high humidity helps to ensure plants are not short of water. Plenty of sunshine and an atmosphere almost free from dust and pollution results in exceptionally high levels of ultraviolet rays. Perhaps it is this intensity of light which produces the famously vivid colours of the islands' flowers.

ALGAE

Algae grow on the shoreline, which is divided into three: the upper, middle and lower shore. The upper shore starts at the high-water mark. The first band of algal growth festooning the rocks is a small brown seaweed appropriately known as **Channel Wrack**. It can withstand long periods out of water, but eventually merges and gives way to Spiral Wrack further down the shore. Here **Purple Laver Weed** can grow. Where freshwater flows over the rocks, it seems to inhibit brown weed, but allows long green strands of soft tubular **Gutweed** to fill the space.

Bladderwrack is often the most dominant seaweed of the middle shore, especially if exposed. On sheltered shores **Knotted Wrack**, the longest lived but least adaptable alga, is often more common. The air bladders of both help these weeds to float clear of being beaten on the rocks by waves. The most abundant green alga here is likely to be bunches of finely branched, feathery **Cladophora**, which can only grow where it is protected by tougher wracks. The **Sea Lettuce** also grows well where protected by brown seaweeds.

Serrated Wrack, which has a saw-tooth edge to its fronds, is the most common seaweed of the lower shore. Tufts of calcareous red algae and **Pepper Dulse** also indicate the start of the red seaweeds, highly shade-tolerant algae capable of living in much deeper water than brown wracks. Red algae are also prone to bleaching in the sun, so they may not always be bright red. In moderately exposed areas, **Thongweed** is common in places and can reach over two metres long in deeper pools or around sheltered rocks.

Five different types of kelp can be found around British shores. The longest, **Sea Belt**, can grow up to four metres long and its holdfast can be bigger than a man's hand. The other common kelp found in Scilly is ***Laminaria digitata***, which is

Rosy garlic

shaped like giant outstretched fingers. Within the dense kelp forests other weeds which survive here include the Thongweed and **Dabberlocks**. This is also where a rare alien, **Captain Pike's Weed**, from the Pacific can be found, which is thought to have arrived on American flying boats during the Second World War.

MOSSES

Several rare mosses have been discovered on the islands, one as recently as 1995. ***Sematophyllum substrumulosum*** grows here on the bark of old Monterey Pine. Outside of Scilly it is also found in the Azores, Canary Islands and Madeira. Many different types of moss grow on the dunes, but the older, Grey Dunes have the best growths.

LIVERWORTS

The rarest liverwort ***Telaranea murphyae*** was probably introduced to Tresco from the southern hemisphere, along with two others, ***Lophocolea semitere*** and ***Lophocolea bispinosa***, which rather strangely can now only be found growing in Scotland. The explanation is that they were all probably imported on exotic trees.

LICHENS

An astonishing number of these primitive plants grow in Scilly. Many lichens are sensitive to atmospheric pollution, so Scilly's clean air allows them to do well. Over 250 different species have so far been discovered. Scilly is the only place in Europe where the **Coralloid Rosette-lichen** grows – on Castle Down, Tresco, St Mary's and St Martin's.

FERNS

Scilly is perhaps unique in that all three species of a rare fern can be found in the islands. None of the adder's-tongue ferns is big or showy, but the rare **Least**, **Small** and **Common Adder's-tongue** all grow here in short turf and damp areas, even occasionally under **Bracken**.

High-water mark lichens – yellow scales   *Serrated wrack*

INTRODUCED WILDLIFE

Since people first visited the islands they have imported many animals and plants, both deliberately and accidentally. In the past cargo stored on foreign soil or left overnight on a beach, may well have collected a tiny stowaway or two. Over the last few thousand years or more, many creatures and wild flowers have undoubtedly found their way to Scilly this way. Trouser turn-ups, rucksacks and handbags can all carry a plant seed or two. Most seeds probably fall on unsuitable soil but just occasionally they are lucky and survive. Other plants and animals were deliberately introduced, some even documented.

Elder trees, which are considered to possess magical powers, were introduced to Scilly sometime after 1120 by the monks of Tavistock. Their growth must have been impressive as Tresco was formerly known as Innischawe, meaning island of the Elder trees.

The South African *Agapanthus*, today found thriving in the islands' dunes, was said to have been established by people scattering its bulbs as they walked around the islands.

But many plants are highly invasive and need little human help. The Hottentot Fig and some of the fleshy leaved Mesembryanthemums can be found on many uninhabited islands. Gulls collecting material for their nests are thought to have carried them to some of the most remote islands in the archipelago. Certainly they can be found growing wherever Gulls nest.

The list of accidental introductions to the islands grows from year to year. They include mosses, liverworts and flowering plants, as well as a tiny land hopper and flatworm from New Zealand. Tresco Gardens has three species of stick insect. The flightless common cockroach also probably arrived in ship's cargo.

Rabbits were first recorded in Britain in 1176, and they were probably already being farmed in Scilly well before then. Today they breed on all the larger islands and many of the smaller uninhabited ones, wherever there is enough greenery.

Some introductions are extraordinary. A red seaweed – *Pikea californica* – is thought to have arrived accidentally from its Pacific Ocean home on the floats of Catalina flying boats. These American aircraft were stationed in the islands during the Second World War.

The deliberate introduction of animals and plants into a small island is today considered to be highly irresponsible, but in the past many creatures were let loose, presumably by people who did not know any better. Luckily most did not survive or have had little impact on the native wildlife of the islands. Colonies of European Tree Frog, Golden Pheasant, Budgerigar and Bobwhite Quail have all been attempted, but perhaps the most serious and potentially destructive was the release of some Hedgehog. Despite their obvious appeal and harmless reputation on the mainland, their introduction to a small island could be highly damaging, as their diet includes bird's eggs. Not only are ground nesting birds such as Terns and Ringed Plover particularly vulnerable, but Hedgehogs are surprisingly good climbers. They can easily reach nests a metre or more above the ground, which could threaten many more species including the Song Thrush. They probably also compete with one of the islands' more famous resident mammals for insect and crustacean food.

FLOWERING PLANTS

In Scilly every season has its floral highlight. By late winter the bulb fields are ablaze with colour. Early spring is when the arable weeds start to flower and on Bryher even **Dwarf Pansy** may be found. By the end of April the first pink splashes of **Thrift** colour the cliffs, while May is **Bluebell** season. The introduced **Spanish Bluebell** with its stout stems and larger blooms appears first, soon followed by the more graceful look-ing native variety. As summer develops, **Foxglove** can be seen rising above **Bramble** or mingled with fragrant **Honeysuckle**. The dandelion-like flowers of **Common Cat's-ear** are a real feature in summer everywhere, tall with hairy leaves and branched stems. In short turf the tiny **Eyebright** also appears around the same time. **Babington's Leek** rear high above dune grasslands and in late summer **Yarrow** look their best with flowers of pink and white on hillsides. Nearer the sea and on cliffs the showy flowering heads of **Wild Carrot** are very distinctive, while **Lesser Hawkbit** have small rosettes of hairy leaves and dandelion-like yellow flowers. In July the **Balm-leaved Figwort** appears, while **Bell Heather**, **Ling** and **Western Gorse** come into flower on the heathlands. Then a beautiful little orchid, the **Autumn Lady's-tresses**, appears almost overnight, often after heavy rain. Whatever the season, Scilly always seems to be blooming.

When compared with mainland Britain, few plants are truly native to the islands, but many introduced exotic ones have become naturalised and now thrive. The **Hottentot Fig** is most commonly found on cliffs. Other members of the same fam-ily include the **Pale Dew Plant** which covers many walls and rocks near the sea. Just as striking are the robust flowering spikes of **Bear's Breeches**, originally from the Mediterranean.

Other escapees from cultivation include **Harlequin Flower**, **Giant Houseleeks** and **Apple of Peru**. The elegant **Agapanthus** or **Blue Lily** from South Africa forms

Below: Bermuda Buttercup. Overleaf: Heather and gorse in full bloom on St Mary's golf course

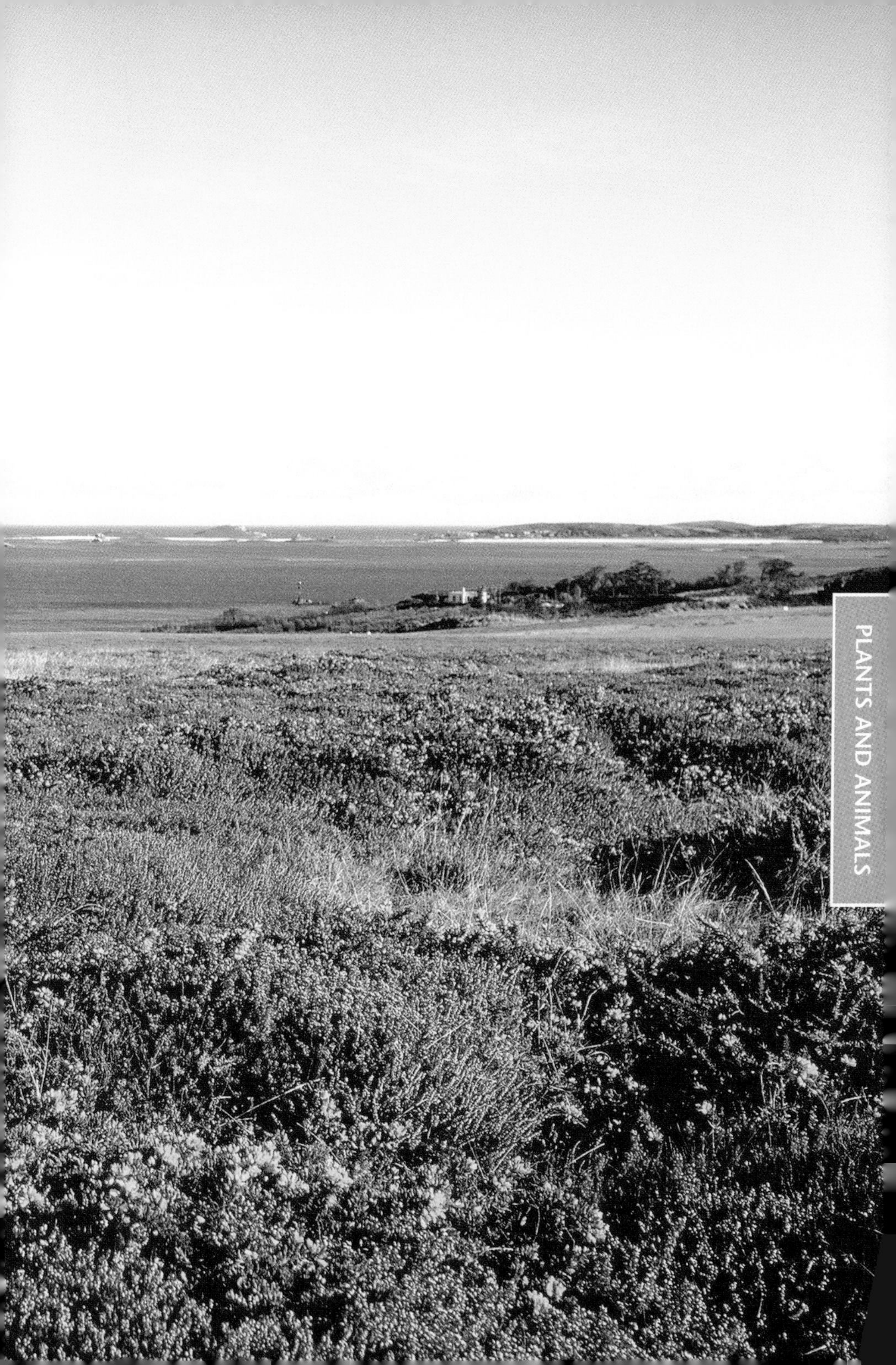

large clumps especially in dunes, and several species of giant **Echium** seed freely in many places. Late in the year the **Pink Lily**, *Amaryllis belladonna*, comes into its own. Locally it is known as **Naked Ladies**, because the flowers appear after the leaves have gone.

Not all these alien plants are welcome in the wild, as many have become weeds. **German Ivy** is found on hedge banks, the **New Zealand Flax** is appearing on cliffs and the **New Zealand Wire Plant** can also withstand salt and wind. Other plants have taken to arable land. One of the most widespread is the bright yellow flower of the **Bermuda Buttercup** – a strange name as it is neither a native of the Caribbean nor a buttercup! It is yellow but comes from South Africa and only opens in full sun. It is a real pest in bulb fields.

Winter Heliotrope grows in damp places along roadsides, soon followed by white-flowered **Three-cornered Leek**. **Celandine** flower in spring along the lanes, along with **Dog Violet**. **Red Campion** is known in Scilly as **Robins**, and can often be found throughout the year. **Rosy Garlic** and **Corn Lily** now also commonly grow on roadsides verges.

To the farmer anything that grows where it is not wanted is a weed, and that includes some native plants such as **Small-flowered Buttercup** and **Small-flowered Catchfly**. In cultivated fields **Corn Marigold, Corn Spurrey, Long-headed Poppy** and **Corn Field Poppy** all seem to flourish.

One of the most difficult to control weeds produces the most spectacular show. The attractive bright yellow Corn Marigold is also known as Bothams and can bloom so profusely that many people mistake it for a crop. Fields of these flowers can look particularly striking where Poppies also grow.

Among the more common arable weeds are the speedwells, **Sow Thistle** and **Chickweed**. Other weeds include **Corn**

Agapanthus   *A variety of the English Catchfly*

PLANTS AND ANIMALS

Salad, **Sheep's Sorrel** and several species of Fumitory.

The **English Catchfly** has two varieties here, one with rose-coloured petals the other with smaller yellowish-white blooms. The **Spotted Catchfly** is white, with a deep red blotch. Once found in bulb fields, today it can probably only be discovered growing in gardens. More often seen are **Lesser Quaking Grass, Field Pennycress, Weasel's Snout** and **Field Woundwort**. A different variety of the **Scarlet Pimpernel**, pale pink and occasionally deep blue, may also be found.

Poppy and **Pink Oxalis** often grow in considerable quantities. The latter is another South African native now found on all the main islands and not just on cultivated land. Other attractive flowers of the field include the aromatic **Musk Stork's-bill, Spotted Medick** and sometimes the yellow-flowered **Toothed Medick**. **Spanish Iris** and **Spanish Bluebell** are now also common in many places.

In spring and summer the wet grasslands are rich in wild flowers, with flourishing stands of **Yellow Iris**, spectacular **Royal Fern** and bright spikes of **Purple Loosestrife**. **Water Mint, Hemlock Water-dropwort** and scattered tufts of **Greater Tussock-sedge** all thrive in such places. Wetter ground supports **Lesser Spearwort** and in small boggy pockets **Bog Pimpernel, Bog Stitchwort** and **Marsh St John's-wort** can grow.

Jointed Orange Bird's-foot

Common Reed fringes the waterside and provides important nesting sites for **Reed and Sedge Warblers**. Freshwater pools and surrounding reed beds are important for migrant as well as breeding birds. They also provide valuable food and shelter for wintering birds and regularly attract rare vagrants.

Heather provides protection for smaller plants. In spring, the heathlands can be alive with the tiny flowers of **Milkwort**. Usually deep blue in colour, they can sometimes be pink or even white in Scilly. Other small flowers include **Lousewort**, **Yellow Tormentil** and **Bird's-foot Trefoil**, which can all be found hiding amongst the rolling waves of heather. Where grassland becomes dominant closer to the cliff edge, **Yorkshire Fog** and **Red Fescue** can be found with magnificent clumps of **Thrift**. In places huge stands of these beautiful pink flowers can cover the cliffs tops and the island of Annet is famed for its colour in early summer.

Dunes provide a habitat for several plants. They are basically arranged in parallel uneven ridges. On the seaward side **Sea Rocket**, **Saltwort**, **Orache** and creeping **Sea Bindweed** may be among the first pioneers to germinate every year. **Sea Spurge** can grow at the top of the shore, while Sea Holly actually needs the tide to disperse its seeds.

But these plants cannot cope with too much sand rising around them. Others can. **Sea Couch Grass** has the ability to grow with a rising dune, at least for a while. Half a metre is its limit; above this height a stronger, more vigorous plant takes over – **Marram**.

Other plants also sometimes appear. Scilly must be one of the few places where **Primroses** regularly flower in the sand and surely the only location where exotic South African **Agapanthus** can be seen in late summer, rising above the Marram. Keep an eye open in the dune slack between the newer Yellow Dune and the more static Fixed Dune for tall, unusual plants such as **Babington's Leek** and **Balm-leaved Figwort**. In the pans where the water table is close to the surface, a swamp can develop, and damp ground is ideal for **Sea Pearlwort**.

Bracken is highly invasive and not a beneficial plant, as it suppresses the growth of other more interesting vegetation nearby. Many islands have been invaded by it, despite efforts to control it. But where Bracken has yet to take root or in places where it is controlled, rabbits nibble the grass and produce a fine turf where some surprisingly tall **Centaury** plants can grow. More interesting are the pale pink flowers of **Sea Stork's-bill**. This is an Atlantic speciality confined to the west coast with rather sticky, undivided leaves. It is smaller than its common cousin, which also grows here.

Scilly is home to three buttercups uncommon on the mainland: **Prickly-fruited, Small-flowered and Hairy Buttercup**. The Prickly-fruited Buttercup is a real Scilly speciality, along with **Western Ramping-fumitory, Smaller Tree Mallow** and **Four-leaved Allseed**. Other national rarities include **Early Meadow-grass, Cretan Mallow, Western Fumitory, Western Clover, Early Meadow Grass** and **Late Cuckoo Pint**.

Notable native wild plants include the **Jointed Orange Bird's-foot** and **Dwarf Pansy**.

Common Centaury

Bird's-foot Trefoil in dunes on St Mary's

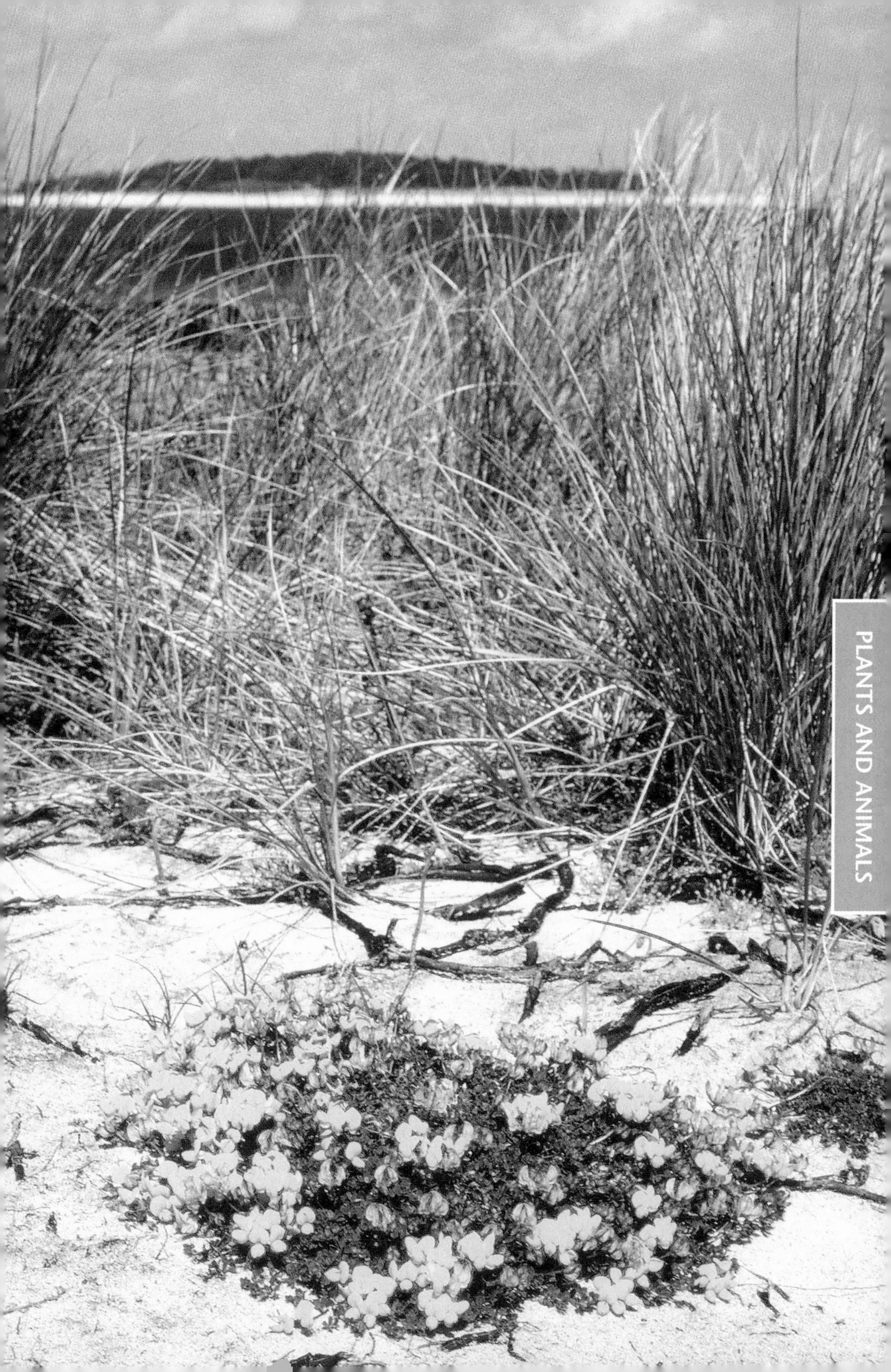

Trees and shrubs

There are few native trees in Scilly. On St Mary's and Tresco, **Elm** is still relatively common, as is **Elder**, but **Oak** and **Blackthorn** are rare. **Hawthorn** is locally scattered on St Mary's and Tresco, as is the **Grey Sallow**, which is also surprisingly found in the Eastern Isles and on St Helen's.

WINDBREAK HEDGES

Most of the hedgerow seen today is probably quite recent, certainly no older than a century or so. Before that stone walls were the first line of defence to protect field crops from the wind. To survive a battering from storms and sea spray takes a hardy kind of plant, and only exotic shrubs seem capable of doing the job. Tough evergreen leaves that can withstand salt-laden winds and strong roots capable of holding on in powerful gusts are the qualities required. Planted around the islands bulb-fields they provide shelter from winter gales but in origin come from far and wide. The most commonly seen include **Pittosporum**, a leathery-leaved plant with small wine-coloured flowers, a native of New Zealand; **Hedge Ragwort**, which is more ornamental than practical; **Escallonia**, with sticky twigs, toothed leaves and attractive pink-red flowers, popular with bees and wasps, a native to the island of Chiloe, off Chile in South America; **Euonymus**, with dark green leaves and greenish-white flowers, a native of southern Japan; and **Hedge Veronica**, with its dense foliage and eye-catching purple flowers, a native of New Zealand.

Less common hedge plants include **Japanese Privet**, which is different from the low-growing Wild Privet; **Coprosma**, a dark green tree with small round shiny leaves and small orange berry fruit, a native of New Zealand; **Olearia**, a silky plant found mainly on Tresco, which come from the Chatham Islands, New Zealand; and **Tamarisk**, an early introduction from the Mediterranean area, now seldom planted as it provides poor shelter. Once used for making lobster-pots. The leaves are tiny and rather greyish scale-like while the conspicuous small pink flowers are grouped together like large catkins.

Elm trees, Dolphin Town , Tresco   *Tamarisk*

PLANTS AND ANIMALS

RARE PLANTS
THAT MAKE SCILLY SPECIAL

Babington's Leek

First discovered on The Lizard in west Cornwall, Babington's Leek is found elsewhere only in western Ireland and south-western England. This rare variety of Wild Leek is a spectacular plant often reaching a dramatic two metres high. A stout perennial with white to purple flowers, it is widespread in Scilly, often found on waste ground, arable fields or old rubbish tips as well as behind sand dunes.

Balm-leaved Figwort

Nationally rare, the Balm-leaved Figwort can grow up to a metre high and is found throughout the islands. It is especially common in stable dune areas where it can be found growing with Marram and Bramble. Its name comes from its toothed, downy-covered leaves, which are borne on square, unwinged stems. While its dull, brown-purple flowers with broad mem-branous margins are not particularly attractive to us, it does have appeal to one insect: the caterpillar of a nationally rare moth, *Nothris congressa,* feasts on its leaves.

Dwarf Pansy

Even by Lilliputian standards this pansy is very small. Easily overlooked, it seldom grows more than 4-8 mm in height, and its exquisite little flowers are beautiful, although you may well need a magnifying glass to really appreciate them.

In the British Isles the Dwarf Pansy is restricted to Scilly and the Channel Islands. First recorded on Tresco in 1873, it is also found on Tean and Bryher. An annual flower, it grows in short-grazed turf on sandy habitats behind dunes, often where the ground is disturbed around rabbit holes or adjacent to small quarries. The flowers appear early, any time from March onwards, before disappearing. In a dry spring they can all vanish by the beginning of May. The biggest colony of some 2,000 plants is to be found on Bryher in the sandy grassland just behind the coastal dunes at Rushy Bay. Increasing disturbance, fewer rabbits and vigorous competition from encroaching Bracken and Gorse have all taken their toll. But their fortunes can change dra-matically. Following the great storms of the winter of 1989/90, when the sea breached and inundated the dunes at Rushy Bay, the sandy grasslands were colonised by huge Dwarf Pansies. Some reached 5 cm wide and over 2 cm high, true giants among

Babington's Leek

dwarfs. It led to a peak population in 1992 of about 20,000 plants. However, within a year Red Fescue and Sand Sedge was forming a dense turf and the numbers of Dwarf Pansy gradually returned to normal. Who would have thought it? What this beautiful little plant really needs is another great storm!

Least Adder's-tongue
The rarest and smallest Adder's-tongue fern in Britain only grows outside mainland Europe in the Channel Islands and on St Agnes in Scilly. It is found on the south side of the island in short turf on shallow soil. It only survives where heathland is rough-grazed and the risk of accidental fires is minimal. A tiny green fern, normally seen only between November and April, it is rarely observed by visitors. It was discovered by chance in March 1950 by botanist John Raven while he was enjoying a sandwich on Wingletang.

Jointed Orange Bird's-foot
In this realm of diminutive plants, the rare Bird's-foot is tiny. Their orange-yellow flowers are borne either singly or in heads of up to five little flowers, barely 6-8 mm long. Low-growing and slender, this plant is almost hairless and usually confined to short maritime or heathy turf. An annual plant, it also sometimes grows on disturbed sandy soil in arable fields or adjacent to sand quarries. Although found on several islands in Scilly, in recent times (on St Mary's) it has only been seen as a garden plant.

Shore Dock
One of the botanical highlights of Scilly, this is the rarest dock in Europe. Yet sadly its future here may be threatened by rising sea levels. In Britain the plant is mainly restricted to coastal locations in south-west England and Wales. Today it is only found on a few islands in Scilly, with fewer than 50 plants growing on even the best sites. So this is a vulnerable plant. It can be found from the strandline to wave-cut platforms, raised beaches and low cliffs. It is often associated with wet flushes and spring seepages. While their numbers are affected by storm damage, there is evidence that some plants have been used to start beach bonfires!

Western Ramping-fumitory
Found only in Scilly and Cornwall, this is the largest of these attractive little flowers, and is still relatively common on St Mary's. Here it can be found scrambling over stone walls, in hedgerows and gardens as well as arable fields. More generally the plant is associated with human activity and soil disturbance.

Balm-leaved Figwort

Plants special to the Isles of Scilly

GARDEN ESCAPES AND ALIEN PLANTS

Name	When in flower	Scilly Status and Country of Origin
Aeonium *Aeonium spp*	July-Nov	Common in gardens. Canary Isles
Agapanthus *Agapanthus praecox*	July-Sept	Frequent on Tresco dunes. South Africa
Apple-of-Peru (Shoo-fly) *Nicandra physalodes*	August	Rare. Peru (poisonous)
Arum Lily *Zantedeschia aethiopica*	April-May	South Africa
Bear's-breeches *Acanthus mollis*	July-Sept	Rare. Mediterranean region
Belladonna Lily *Amaryllis belladonna*	Sept-Nov	Common. South Africa
Bermuda Buttercup *Oxalis pes-caprae*	Mar-May	Common in bulb fields. South Africa
Evening Primrose *Oenothera glazioviana*	July-Aug	Common on St Mary's and Tresco in dunes. North America
German Ivy *Delairea Odorata*	Jan-Feb	South Africa
Hedge Veronica *Hebe lewisii*	June-July	Common windbreak. New Zealand
Hottentot Fig *Carpobrotus edulis*	May-June	Abundant on coast. South Africa
Japanese Knotweed *Fallopia cuspidatum*	Aug-Sept	Local on main islands. Japan
Libertia Formosa	April-May	Chile
Montbretia *Crocosmia x crocosmiflora*	July-Aug	South Africa
New Zealand Flax *Phormium tenax*	June-July	New Zealand
Pigweed *Amaranthus retroflexus*	July-Sept	Locally common. North America
Pittosporum *Pittosporum crassifolium*	May	Common as hedge. New Zealand
Prickly-fruited Buttercup *Ranunculus muricatus*	May-June	Common in bulb fields. Southern Europe
Salsola kali	July-Sept	Rare, beach strandline.
Red Valerian *Centranthus ruber*	June-Aug	Locally common on St Mary's. Mediterranean region
Rosy Garlic *Allium roseum*	May-June	Mediterranean region
Spring Beauty *Claytonia (Montia) perfoliata*	May-July	Common in bulb fields. North America
Spring Snowflake *Leucojum vernum*	Mar-April	Mediterranean region
Spring Starflower *Ipheion uniflorum*	Mar-April	South America
Tamarisk *Tamarix gallica*	June-Aug	Common. Mediterranean region
Thorn Apple *Datura stramonium*	July-Oct	America (poisonous)
Tree Echium *E. pininana**	May-June	Canary Islands
Tree Lupin *Lupinus arboreus*	May-Aug	California
Watsonia borbonica	May-June	South Africa
Whistling Jacks *Gladiolus byzantinus*	April-May	Mediterranean region

*(plus hybrids *x scillionensis*)

Bear's-breeches

|144|

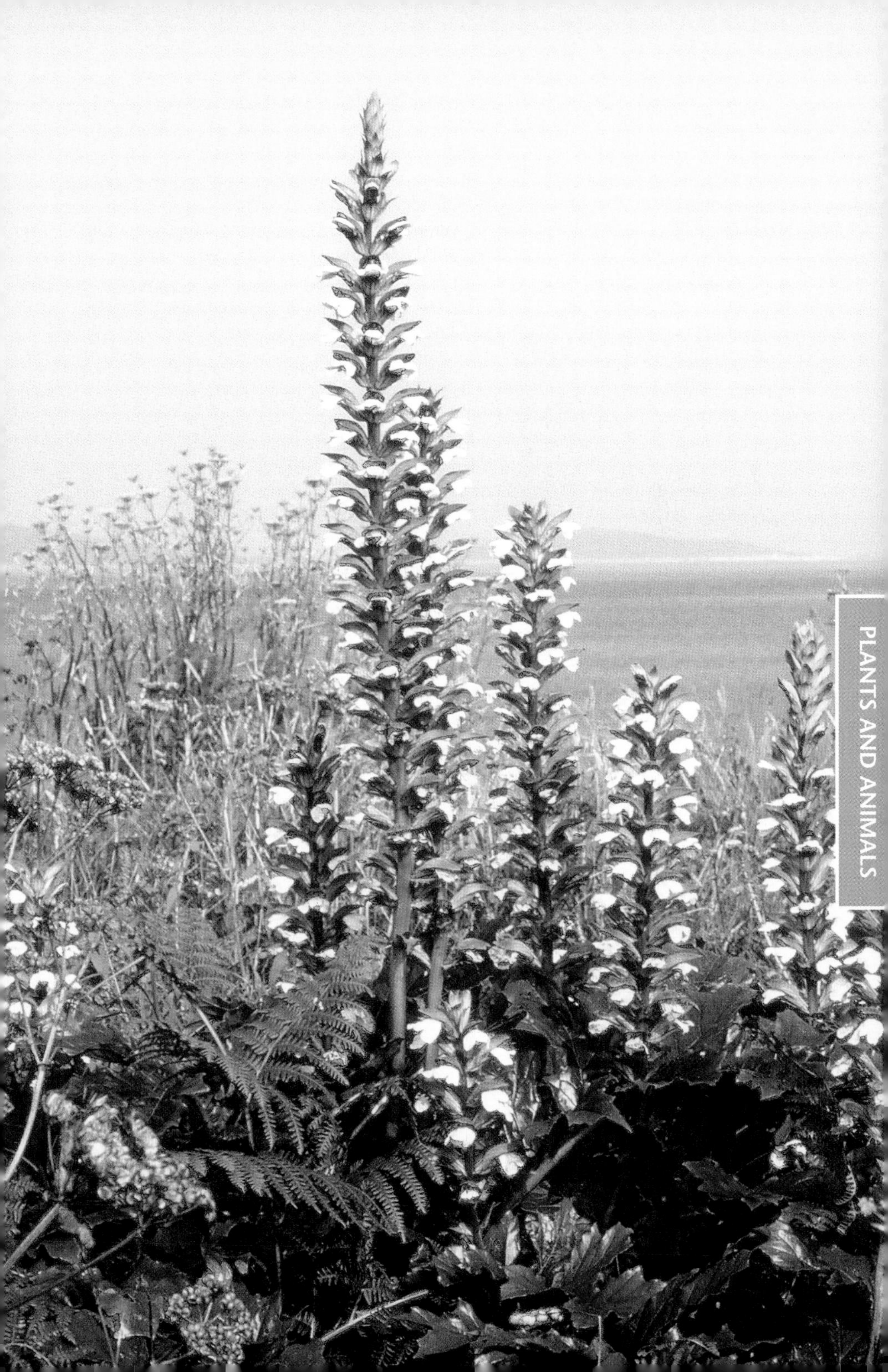

NATIONALLY RARE PLANTS

Name	When in flower	Scilly Status and Country of origin
Babington's Leek *Allium ampeloprasum var. babingtonii*	July-Aug	Frequent. Dune grassland and fallow fields
Chamomile *Chamaemelum nobile*	July-Sept	Common. Heathland
Balm-leaved Figwort *Scrophularia scorodonia*	June-Aug	Abundant. Dune grassland
Common Cudweed *Filago vulgaris*	July-Aug	Frequent on St Mary's and St Agnes. Roadside and cultivated fields
Dwarf Pansy *Viola kitaibeliana*	April-July	Scarce. Dune grassland
Early Meadow-grass *Poa infirma*	Mar-May	Frequent. Maritime grassland
Four-leaved Allseed *Polycarpon tetraphyllum*	June-July	Common. Bulb and arable fields
Hairy Bird's-foot Trefoil *Lotus subbiflorus*	June-Sept	Uncommon. Field and waste ground
Jointed Orange Bird's-foot *Ornithopus pinnatus*	April-Aug	Frequent. Maritime grassland and heathland
Least Adder's-tongue fern *Ophioglossum lusitanicum*	Feb-April	Very rare. Maritime grassland and heathland on St Agnes
Shepherd's needle *Scandix pecten-veneris*	June-July	Rare. Arable
Small Tree or Cretan Mallow *Lavatera cretica*	June-July	Frequent on St Mary's Tresco and St Agnes. Arable and bulb fields
Shore Dock *Rumex rupestris*	June-Aug	Very Rare. Beaches
Small Adder's-tongue *Ophioglossum azoricum*	Appears April	Rare. Maritime grassland and heathland
Western Clover *Trifolium occidentale*	Mar-May	Common, main islands. Maritime grassland
Western Ramping-fumitory *Fumaria occidentalis*	April-Oct	Locally plentiful. Hedge banks, bulb and arable fields
Wild Leek *Allium ampeloprasum*	June-Aug	St Mary's

Fumitory　　　　　　　　　　　　　　　　　　　　　　　　　　　*Dwarf pansy*

Birds

Breeding birds

Scilly has relatively few resident birds compared with similar-sized areas on the mainland. Breeding birds consist mainly of a mixture of resident and regular summer visitors. Apart from two waders and 15 seabirds, less than 50 other birds are known to nest in the islands. Most woodland birds found on the mainland do not breed in Scilly, although good numbers migrate through the islands each year. There are no resident magpies, owls, woodpeckers or jays.

Some breeding seabirds, such as the **Storm Petrel** and perhaps the **Manx Shearwater**, are of national importance. Both are summer visitors, spending the rest of the year out to sea, perhaps as far away as the South Atlantic. Both breed in holes, only coming ashore after dark. Storm Petrels nest in large colonies between boulders at the back of rocky beaches, their calls merging to sound like a factory of sewing machines underground. Their population is difficult to estimate but there are thought to be around 2,000-3,000 pairs. Shearwaters breed in burrows in the turf and their weird choking calls have terrorised sailors for centuries. By day both petrels and shearwaters fish far from shore. Evening is the best time to catch a glimpse of the Manx Shearwater as they assemble in rafts, and special boat trips are arranged in midsummer to find them. Being oceanic birds, they are vulnerable to attack on land and their greatest threat comes from large gulls.

Herring Gull, Great and Lesser Black-backed Gulls all breed on the uninhabited islands. The colonies of Lesser Black-backed gulls are big: Samson and Gugh contain over

Razorbill   *Shag heading for fishing ground*
Overleaf: Great Black-backed Gull chick with egg

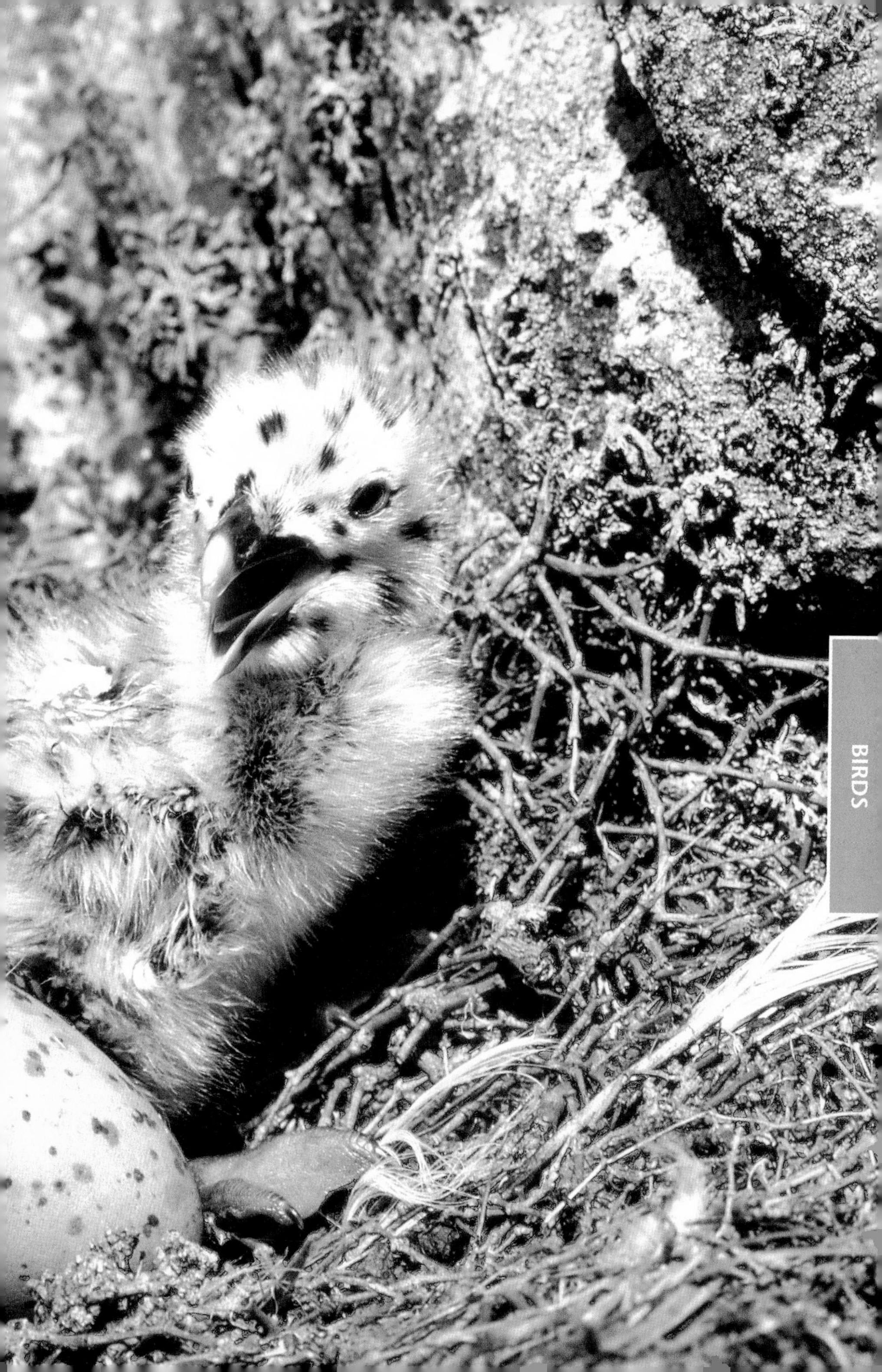

1,000 pairs each and Annet a few less. St Helen's now has a large colony which may be growing at the expense of the Eastern Isles, where perhaps less than 100 pairs now breed. Lesser Black-backed Gulls mainly scavenge for small food picked from the sea. In contrast the Herring and Great Black-backed Gulls are formidable predators, stealing eggs and young given half a chance. The Great Black-backed Gulls especially prey on fledgling birds and may also rob adult birds of their food.

The attractive **Kittiwake** nests on several unusually low cliff sites around the islands. **Common Tern** breed most years, but **Sandwich Tern** and the rare **Roseate Tern** have had little success in recent times. Terns are fickle birds, easily disturbed, and their colonies in Scilly over the last decade appear to be rather tenuous. Fortunately some can still be seen off the beaches in summer, spectacularly hovering and diving into the water for small fish, especially in Tresco Channel.

Guillemot, Razorbill and **Puffin** are often known simply as Auks. All three are present from early spring until July on some of the most inaccessible rocks but none in big numbers. In 1908 it was estimated that up to 100,000 Puffin were breeding in Scilly, yet by the end of the Second World War barely twenty pairs could be counted. Since then numbers have fluctuated, and today they might reach over 160 pairs, having remained relatively static over the past decade or so. The decline is thought to be linked to predation by rats and **Great Black-backed Gulls**. More likely the reason is not so simple, and the varying population of their principal food, sand eels, may have played a part.

The **Fulmar** is an oceanic bird for much of the year, but nests on rock stacks and cliffs. Resident **Oystercatcher** and **Ringed Plover** tend to choose the most undisturbed rocky and sandy bays. Only about 50 pairs of **Cormorant** breed in the islands. They are greatly outnumbered by a smaller relative that also stands on rocks with wings outstretched to dry, the **Shag**. This bird is most obvious when they collect in large fishing flocks of up to 300, flying low over the water searching for shoals of small fish. Over 500 pairs are known to nest on the Western Rocks alone.

Other birds here can be found on farmland in far higher densities than on the mainland. In Scilly the **Blackbird, Robin** and **Song Thrush** are all remarkably unafraid of people. **House Sparrows** also seem to be everywhere on the inhabited islands, thriving here while many mainland populations struggle. They too appear tame, perhaps because of the absence of mammalian predators, although cats and increasing numbers of introduced hedgehogs may be taking their toll. Apart from scavenging gulls, birds of prey are the only other predators, and most are visitors. However, at least one pair of **Kestrel** is resident in the islands and one pair of **Peregrine** seems to regularly produce a brood.

Rock Pipit breed on all the major islands. A rather drab little bird, it hides its nest well. It needs to, because they are a favoured host for the cuckoo between late April and early July. Another small bird, the **Wren**, has a call completely out of proportion to its size: its explosive song from a bush close to a footpath often startles passers-by. Wrens do not travel far, and Scillonian Wrens have even been described as a distinct island race. They do indeed appear bigger, bolder and more rusty-coloured than any found on the mainland.

Common Tern

BIRDS

Migrant birds

Scilly must be one of the most popular and exciting places for bird-watching anywhere in Britain. Remarkably, these tiny islands have given rise to the greatest proportion of extreme rarities recorded in the British Isles. 'First seen in Scilly' is an all too common note against many of the UK's rarest vagrant birds. For many keen birders, the annual October odyssey to Scilly is a firm date in their diaries.

Autumn is best, but spring can also bring surprises. The variety of birds that appear from places as widespread as Asia and America has to be seen to be believed. Apart from the excitement of discovering birds that have strayed thousands of miles off their normal course, their guest appearance is tangible evidence of the sheer scale of bird movements worldwide. Every year millions of birds migrate around the globe, mainly unseen. Many fly vast distances across mountain, desert and sea. For some their journey is of epic, mind-blowing distances, like the Arctic Tern that regularly travels from pole to pole, not once but twice a year.

Not all visiting birds are rare vagrants. Many regular migrants pass through the islands before heading for the distant mainland. There is no better thrill than seeing summer arrive in the form of a dashing flock of **Swallow** speeding across the waves, winging up over the islands before heading for the Cornish mainland. Even more memorable was an encounter I had with a bird so familiar that everyone can recognise its call, yet few people can claim to have actually seen one. Somewhere out to sea off St Agnes, I heard a **Cuckoo** calling louder and louder as it approached land. A stiffening headwind made its progress more difficult. Finally it alighted, breathless, on a boulder surrounded by pink Thrift. A picture of relief, it rested for a while oblivious to my human presence. Its long journey had no doubt been fraught with danger. Flying from central Africa, through tropical storms raging above rainforest, across parched sands from oasis to oasis, it eventually crossed the Straits of Gibraltar. Passing through olive groves and mountain passes, avoiding guns, nets and snares, the English Channel was its last hurdle. Carried on a brisk southerly breeze a cuckoo may easily manage several hundred miles a day. But if the wind backs suddenly, it can quickly become a fight for survival. Every year countless birds die on migration. But for one exhausted Cuckoo, the Isles of Scilly loomed just in time. Although a few breed on the islands, most just pass through. Such is the excitement of Scilly birding.

Bird-watching can even begin before you arrive. If you are arriving by boat, look out for seabirds during your journey such as **Gannet**, **Fulmar**, **Shearwater**, **Grey Phalarope**, **Auks** and **Skuas**. Even from the air, aboard the helicopter or Skybus, gulls and Gannets can easily be seen. The spring migration begins as early as March. The arrival of **Meadow Pipit** and perhaps the first **White Wagtail** signals the start, before **Wheatear** and **Sandwich Tern** begin to appear. Early April usually heralds an influx of **Willow Warblers**, often in their hundreds. More difficult to find but almost as regular is the near annual guest appearance of the exotic-looking **Hoopoe**. The month that follows is a busy one for the Scilly birder as migrants arrive thick and fast in bright spring plumage and full song.

A fair wind can bring in even more interesting migrants. Up to five different herons may appear as well as **Golden Oriole**, **Spotted Flycatcher** and **Turtle Dove**.

Common Snipe

Even **Bee-eaters** are seen occasionally. **Swallow** and **Martin**, then **Swift** usually put on a fleeting show chasing insects over the pools. The middle of May is always a good time for spring migrants. Many will be continental birds overshooting their destinations. **Red-rumped Swallow, Purple and Night Heron** are no strangers to Scillonian shores early in the year.

It hardly seems that summer is underway before migrants begin to return from the north. The end of July finds **Greenshank** and **Redshank** along with some **Sandpiper** back on the shores. Then bird numbers begin to build as the autumn migration really gets into gear. Waders and warblers, flycatchers and chats can be joined by transatlantic visitors if a west wind blows by the end of August. Autumn usually sees the first American waders arrive, often the **Pectoral Sandpiper**. Once regular but now declining, the occasional **Buff-breasted Sandpiper** puts in an appearance at the island airport, feeding in the short turf.

Some birds are more predictable than others. Scilly is one of the best places to get close to **Common and Jack Snipe**, and **Wryneck** can be surprisingly numerous, along with **Common Rosefinch, Ortolan** and **Lapland Bunting, Melodious** and **Icterine Warbler, Bluethroat** and possibly a **Pectoral Sandpiper** eagerly feeding alongside a pool.

While more common species come and go during September, October offers the chance of finding a real rarity. It is the height of the Scilly birding season. Weather fronts sweep in across the Atlantic bringing changeable winds, east one day, west the next, then north or maybe south. As millions of migrating birds battle against inclement conditions or take advantage of a good breeze, the islands briefly become a mecca for birds and watchers alike. **Firecrest** and **Yellow-browed Warbler** can become almost common for a few days, and birders become blasé about **Red-breasted Flycatcher**.

This month also offers perhaps the best chance in Britain of seeing a **Red-eyed Vireo** or **Rose-breasted Grosbeak**. Long grass may hide a **Richard's Pipit** or two keeping their heads down, especially if a visiting bird of prey passes through. Pipits come high on the menu of the fleet-flying **Merlin**. The resident Kestrel are joined by migrating kin, while Peregrine and Sparrowhawk seem easier than usual to approach. Add the **Short-eared Owl** and **Hen Harrier**, and October ends in a fitting finale to one of the greatest bird shows on earth.

The famously mild winter weather allows some summer visiting birds to linger longer in Scilly than on the mainland. **Swallow** and **House Martin** often stay into November and even December, while others may remain throughout winter. Offshore, the **Great Northern Diver** are a seasonal treat, with even **Long-tailed Duck** being reported. **Goldcrest** and **Chiffchaff** are not uncommon during the coldest months, with the occasional **Blackcap** and **Firecrest**. **Black Redstart** may be found down in sheltered coves while the mainland shivers in snow.

In the depths of winter a severe cold spell across the UK can see a mass migration of birds south and west. Scilly is internationally recognised as a major wintering area for wading birds. It is not unusual to find large numbers of wildfowl as well as **Fieldfare, Redwing, Lapwing, Golden Plover** and **Meadow Pipit**, along with a few **Woodcock** and **Snipe**, all sheltering there.

From the end of August until mid-May, most wading birds are down on the

Overleaf: Puffin and Guillemot on Men-a-vaur

shore. **Sanderling** and **Turnstone** are relatively easy to find, while the piping call of the **Oystercatcher** is the most common sound of the coast. **Purple Sandpiper** can be seen on the seaward side of St Mary's Quay and probably more on St Agnes. **Grey Heron** and **Little Egret** can usually be seen wading in the shallows of undisturbed bays. The Egret is now commonly found off St Mary's and around Tresco from the end of July through to May. Once a rare vagrant, they are now semi-resident in the islands. At high tide when their feeding grounds are flooded, they roost in small groups, mainly in Tresco Sound and Great Pool. Numbers reduce in late spring, and they are usually absent from the islands in early summer. Perhaps one day they will stay and breed. Now that really would look exotic!

In Scilly every season has its highlight, and every day is different. The bird list for the islands grows year by year. Few other places in Britain can match the extraordinary diversity of migrants and rare vagrants, and few other places can boast such a concentration of skilled birders, binoculars and scopes. Whatever the season, birding in Scilly is always exciting.

Redshank

BIRDS

An alphabetical check list of
birds on the Isles of Scilly

Up to 250 different birds are seen in Scilly most years. The current official list is impressive, containing some 426 birds, and every year it seems to grow. Some breeding birds are of national importance. What follows is a comprehensive but not definitive list. It includes most of the birds recorded in Scilly from 1950 until 2003 in alphabetical order. The common names are those used in most up-to-date bird identification guides but occasional variances may occur. If in doubt, please refer to the scientific name.

As a guide, the following table indicates the criteria used for the various status descriptions.

	Approximate annual numbers	
	Non-breeding birds	Breeding pairs
Very common	>2000	>1000
Common	1001-2000	501-1000
Fairly Common	251-1000	126-500
Uncommon	51-250	26-125
Fairly Rare	11-50	6-25
Rare	1-10	0.5-5
Very rare	<1	<0.5

Those species that have been recorded at sea, but not from the land, are *italicised*. Resident birds may be assumed to breed.
Birds that are regularly seen in Scilly are in blue.

Sightings of some rare birds, marked 'R' in the table, require a National Rarities description to be accepted. Others, marked 'S', require a full description for acceptance in the Isles of Scilly official bird list. Those marked 'I 'are introduced species.

Sanderling

Birds of Scilly

Name		Status & when seen
Alpine Accentor *Prunella collaris*	R	Very rare autumn migrant
Alpine Swift *Apus melba*	R	Very rare migrant
American Black Duck *Anas rubripes*	R	Very rare migrant, occasional resident
American Golden Plover *Pluvialis dominica*	R	Rare, mainly autumn migrant
American Herring Gull *Larus a. smithsonianus*	R	Very rare winter visitor
American Marsh Hawk *Circus cyaneus hudsonius*	R	Very rare migrant
American Purple Gallinule *Porphyrula martinica*	R	Very rare autumn migrant
American Robin *Turdus migratorius*	R	Very rare autumn migrant
American Wigeon *Anas americana*	S	Very rare autumn migrant
Aquatic Warbler *Acrocephalus paludicola*	S	Very rare autumn migrant
Arctic Redpoll *Carduelis hornemanni*	R	Very rare, mainly autumn migrant and a spring record
Arctic Skua *Stercorarius parasiticus*		Fairly rare, mainly autumn migrant
Arctic Tern *Sterna paradisaea*		Rare, mainly autumn migrant
Arctic Warbler *Phylloscopus borealis*	R	Very rare autumn migrant
Ashy-headed Wagtail *Motacilla flava*	S	Very rare spring migrant
Avocet *Recurvirostra avosetta*		Rare migrant, very rare winter visitor
Baird's Sandpiper *Calidris bairdii*	R	Very rare autumn migrant
Balearic Shearwater *Puffinus mauretanicus*		Fairly rare, mainly autumn migrant
Baltimore Oriole *Icterus galbula*	R	Very rare autumn migrant
Barn Owl *Tyto alba*	S	Very rare autumn migrant and winter visitor
Barnacle Goose *Branta leucopsis*		Rare autumn migrant
Barred Warbler *Sylvia nisoria*	S	Rare autumn migrant
Bar-tailed Godwit *Limosa lapponica*		Fairly rare autumn and winter migrant, but good spring passage in late April and May
Bearded Tit *Panurus biarmicus*	S	Rare autumn migrant
Bee-eater *Merops apiaster*	S	Rare, mainly spring migrant
Bewick's Swan *Cygnus columbianus*		Very rare winter migrant
Bicknell's Thrush *Catharus minimus bicknelli*	R	Very rare autumn migrant
Bimaculated Lark *Malanocorypha bimaculata*	R	Very rare autumn migrant
Bittern *Botaurus stellaris*	S	Very rare autumn migrant and winter visitor
Black-and-White Warbler *Mniotilta varia*	R	Very rare autumn migrant
Black Giullemot *Cepphus grylle*	S	Very rare spring migrant
Black Kite *Milvus migrans*	R	Rare, mainly spring migrant

Name		Status & when seen
Black Redstart *Phoenicurus ochruros*		Uncommon, mainly autumn migrant and rare winter visitor
Black Stork *Ciconia nigra*	R	Very rare migrant
Black Tern *Chlidonias niger*		Rare migrant
Black-billed Cuckoo *Coccyzus erythrophthalmus*	R	Very rare autumn migrant
Blackbird *Turdus merula*		Very common resident
Black-browed Albatross *Thalassarche melanophris*	R	Very rare migrant
Blackcap *Sylvia atricapilla*		Uncommon, mainly autumn migrant. Fairly rare breeder, rare summer & winter visitor
Black-headed Bunting *Emberiza melanocephala*	R	Very rare migrant
Black-headed Gull *Larus ridibundus*		Fairly common winter migrant and seen all year, except May and June
Black-necked Grebe *Podiceps nigricollis*	S	Very rare winter migrant
Blackpoll Warbler *Dendroica striata*	R	Very rare autumn migrant
Black-tailed Godwit *Limosa limosa*		Fairly rare, mainly spring and autumn migrant
Black-throated Diver *Gavia arctica*	S	Rare winter migrant
Black-winged Stilt *Himantopus himantopus*	R	Very rare winter migrant, but one spring and one summer record
Blue Rock Thrush *Monticola solitarius*	R	Very rare autumn migrant
Blue Tit *Parus caeruleus*		Fairly common resident. Fairly rare winter migrant
Blue-cheeked Bee-eater *Merops superciliosus*	R	Very rare spring migrant
Blue-headed Wagtail *Motacilla flava flava*		Rare migrant
Bluethroat *Luscinia svecica*	S	Rare migrant
Blue-winged Teal *Anas discors*	R	Very rare autumn migrant
Blyth's Pipit *Anthus godlewskii*	R	Very rare autumn migrant
Blyth's Reed Warbler *Acrocephalus dumetorum*	R	Very rare autumn migrant
Bobolink *Dolichonyx oryzivorus*	R	Very rare autumn migrant
Bonaparte's Gull *Larus philadelphia*	R	Very rare migrant
Booted Warbler *Hippolais caligata*	R	Very rare autumn migrant
Brambling *Fringill montifringilla*		Uncommon, mainly autumn migrant. Rare winter visitor
Bridled Tern *Sterna anaethetus*	R	Very rare summer migrant
Brown Shrike *Lanius cristatus*	R	Very rare autumn migrant
Buff-bellied Pipit *Anthus rubescens*	R	Very rare autumn migrant
Buff-breasted Sandpiper *Tryngites subruficollis*	S	Rare, mainly autumn migrant
Bullfinch *Pyrrhula pyrrhula*		Rare winter migrant, also seen spring and autumn
Buzzard *Buteo buteo*		Rare migrant. Very rare winter visitor
Calandra Lark *Malanocorypha calandra*	R	Very rare spring migrant
Canada Goose *Branta canadensis*	I	Fairly rare resident
Carrion Crow *Corvus corone*		Fairly rare resident
Caspian Plover *Charadrius asiaticus*	R	Very rare spring migrant
Cattle Egret *Bubulcus ibis*	R	Very rare spring migrant
Cetti's Warbler *Cettia cettia*	S	Very rare winter migrant

Birds of Scilly *(continued)*

Name		Status & when seen
Chaffinch *Fringilla coelebs*		Common, mainly autumn migrant. Uncommon resident
Chiffchaff *Phylloscopus collybita*		Common migrant, uncommon summer breeder. Fairly rare winter visitor
Chimney Swift *Chaetura pelagica*	R	Very rare autumn migrant
Chough *Pyrrhocorax pyrrhocorax*	S	Very rare migrant
Cirl Bunting *Emberiza cirlus*		Very rare winter visitor
Citrine Wagtail *Motacilla citreola*	R	Rare autumn migrant and spring 2005
Cliff Swallow *Hirundo pyrrhonota*	R	Very rare autumn migrant
Coal Tit *Parus ater*	S	Rare autumn migrant & winter visitor
Collared Dove *Streptopelia decaocto*		Uncommon resident. Rare migrant
Collared Flycatcher *Ficedula albicollis*	R	Very rare spring migrant
Collared Pratincole *Glareola pratincola*	R	Very rare spring migrant
Common Gull *Larus canus*		Fairly rare, mainly autumn migrant & winter visitor
Common Rosefinch *Carpodacus erythrinus*	S	Rare, mainly autumn migrant
Common Sandpiper *Actitis hypoleucos*		Uncommon autumn migrant, quite common spring
Common Scoter *Melanitta nigra*		Rare winter migrant
Common Tern *Sterna hirundo*		Uncommon breeder & summer visitor. Fairly rare migrant
Coot *Fulica atra*		Uncommon winter migrant. Rare resident
Cormorant *Phalacrocorax carbo*		Uncommon resident
Corn Bunting *Miliaria calandra*	S	Very rare, mainly spring migrant
Corncrake *Crex crex*	S	Rare migrant
Cory's Shearwater *Calonectris diomedea*		Uncommon autumn migrant
Crane *Grus grus*	S	Very rare migrant & summer visitor
Crested Tit *Parus cristatus*	S	Very rare autumn migrant
Crossbill *Loxia curvirostra*		Fairly rare autumn migrant. Very rare winter visitor & spring migrant
Cuckoo *Cuculus canorus*		Fairly rare breeder, summer visitor & migrant
Curlew *Numenius arquata*		Uncommon but seen all months except May and June
Curlew Sandpiper *Calidris ferruginea*		Fairly rare, mainly autumn migrant
Dark-bellied Brent Goose *Branta bernicla bernicla*		Rare winter migrant
Dark-breasted Barn Owl *Tyto alba guttata*	S	Very rare autumn migrant
Dark-throated Thrush *Turdus ruficollis*	R	Very rare autumn migrant
Dartford Warbler *Sylvia undata*	S	Very rare, mainly autumn migrant
Desert Wheatear *Oenanthe deserti*	R	Very rare spring migrant
Dotterel *Charadrius morinellus*		Rare migrant
Dunlin *Calidris alpina*		Uncommon migrant
Dunnock *Prunella modularis*		Common resident
Dusky Warbler *Phylloscopus fuscatus*	R	Very rare autumn migrant
Eastern Black-eared Wheatear *Oenanthe hispanica melanoleuca*	R	Very rare migrant

BIRDS

Birds of Scilly (continued)

Name		Status & when seen
Eastern Bonelli's Warbler *Phylloscopus orientalis*	R	Very rare autumn migrant
Eastern Olivaceous Warbler *Hippolais pallida*	R	Very rare autumn migrant
Eastern Stonechat *Saxicola torquata maura*	R	Very rare, mainly autumn migrant
Eider *Somateria mollissima*	S	Rare migrant. Very rare winter visitor
European White-fronted Goose *Anser albifrons albifrons*		Very rare autumn migrant
Eye-browed Thrush *Turdus obscurus*	R	Very rare autumn migrant
Feral Pigeon (Rock Dove) *Columba livia*		Uncommon resident
Ferruginous Duck *Aythya nyroca*	R	Very rare winter and spring migrant
Fieldfare *Turdus pilaris*		Fairly common, mainly autumn migrant & winter visitor
Firecrest *Regulus ignicapilla*		Uncommon, mainly autumn migrant. Rare winter visitor
Fulmar *Fulmarus glacialis*		Fairly common breeder, summer visitor & winter migrant
Gadwall *Anas strepera*		Uncommon resident & migrant
Gannet *Morus bassanus*		Very common summer visitor & winter migrant
Garden Warbler *Sylvia borin*		Uncommon, mainly autumn migrant
Garganey *Anas querquedula*		Rare migrant
Glaucous Gull *Larus hyperboreus*	S	Rare winter migrant
Glossy Ibis *Plegadis falcinellis*	R	Very rare migrant
Goldcrest *Regulus regulus*		Fairly common, mainly autumn migrant: Fairly rare winter visitor. Rare breeder & summer visitor
Golden Oriole *Oriolus oriolus*		Fairly rare, mainly spring migrant
Golden Plover *Pluvialis apricaria*		Uncommon migrant. Fairly rare winter visitor
Goldeneye *Bucephala clangula*		Rare winter visitor
Goldfinch *Carduelis carduelis*		Fairly common migrant. Fairly rare breeder. Summer & winter visitor
Goosander *Mergus merganser*		Very rare winter visitor
Goshawk *Accipiter gentilis*	S	Very rare autumn migrant
Grasshopper Warbler *Locustella naevia*		Fairly rare, mainly spring migrant
Great Black-backed Gull *Larus marinus*		Common resident
Great Crested Grebe *Podiceps cristatus*		Very rare winter migrant
Great Egret *Ardea alba*	R	Very rare spring migrant
Great Grey Shrike *Lanius excubitor*	S	Very rare winter migrant, also seen autumn

Manx shearwater flying at sunset

Name	Status & when seen
Great Northern Diver *Gavia immer*	Rare winter migrant
Great Reed Warbler *Acrocephalus arundinaceus* R	Very rare, mainly spring migrant
Great Shearwater *Puffinis gravis*	Fairly rare autumn migrant
Great Skua *Catharacta skua*	Fairly rare, mainly autumn migrant
Great Snipe *Gallinago media* R	Very rare autumn migrant
Great Spotted Cuckoo *Clamator glandarius* R	Very rare spring migrant
Great Spotted Woodpecker *Dendrocopos major*	Very rare autumn migrant & winter visitor
Great Tit *Parus major*	Uncommon resident. Fairly rare spring & winter migrant
Greater Yellowlegs *Tringa melanoleuca* R	Very rare autumn migrant
Green Sandpiper *Tringa ochropus*	Fairly rare, mainly autumn migrant
Green Warbler *Phylloscopus t. nitidus* R	Very rare autumn migrant
Greenfinch *Carduelis chloris*	Fairly common, mainly autumn migrant, uncommon breeder, summer & winter visitor
Greenish Warbler *Phylloscopus trochiloides* R	Very rare, mainly autumn migrant
Greenland Wheatear *Oenanthe o. leucorhoa*	Rare, mainly spring migrant
Greenland White-fronted Goose *Anser albifrons flavirostris*	Rare, mainly autumn migrant
Greenshank *Tringa nebularia*	Uncommon, mainly autumn migrant: Rare winter visitor
Green-winged Teal *Anas carolinenesis*	Very rare, mainly autumn migrant & winter visitor
Grey Heron *Ardea cinerea*	Fairly rare resident & migrant
Grey Phalarope *Phalaropus fulicarius*	Fairly rare autumn migrant. Rare winter visitor
Grey Plover *Pluvialis squatarola*	Fairly rare winter migrant
Grey Wagtail *Motacilla cinerea*	Uncommon, mainly autumn migrant. Rare winter visitor
Grey-cheeked Thrush *Catharus minimus* R	Very rare autumn migrant
Grey-headed Wagtail *Motacilla flava thunbergi* S	Very rare migrant
Greylag Goose *Anser anser*	Rare winter migrant
Guillemot *Uria aalge*	Fairly common breeder, summer visitor & winter migrant
Gull-billed Tern *Sterna nilotica* R	Very rare spring migrant
Gyr Falcon *Falco rusticolus* R	Very rare autumn, winter and spring migrant
Hawfinch *Coccothraustes coccothraustes*	Rare, mainly autumn migrant
Hen Harrier *Circus cyaneus*	Rare winter migrant
Hermit Thrush *Catharus guttatus* R	Very rare autumn migrant

Birds of Scilly (continued)

Name		Status & when seen
Herring Gull *Larus argentatus argenteus*		Common resident
Hobby *Falco subbuteo*		Rare migrant
Honey Buzzard *Pernis apivorus*	S	Very rare, mainly autumn migrant
Hooded Crow *Corvus cornix*		Rare migrant
Hooded Warbler *Wilsonia citrina*	R	Very rare autumn migrant
Hoopoe *Upupa epops*		Fairly rare, mainly spring migrant
House Martin *Delichon urbica*		Common Migrant. Rare breeder & summer visitor
House Sparrow *Passer domesticus*		Common resident
Hume's Warbler *Phylloscopus humei*	R	Very rare autumn migrant
Iberian Chiffchaff *Phylloscopus ibericus*	R	Very rare spring migrant
Iceland Gull *Larus glaucoides*	S	Rare winter visitor
Icterine Warbler *Hippolais icterina*	S	Fairly rare autumn migrant
Isabelline Shrike *Lanius isabellinus*	R	Very rare autumn migrant
Isabelline Wheatear *Oenanthe isabellina*	R	Very rare autumn migrant
Jack Snipe *Lymnocryptes minimus*		Fairly rare migrant. Rare winter visitor
Jackdaw *Corvus monedula*		Fairly rare winter migrant. Rare resident
Jay *Garrulus glandarius*	S	Very rare migrant
Kentish Plover *Charadrius alexandrinus*	S	Very rare migrant
Kestrel *Falco tinnunculus*		Fairly rare resident
Killdeer *Charadrius vociferus*	R	Very rare, mainly autumn migrant & winter visitor
Kingfisher *Alcedo atthis*		Fairly rare, mainly autumn migrant. Rare winter visitor
Kittiwake *Rissa tridactyla*		Fairly common winter migrant. Fairly common summer breeder
Knot *Calidris canutus*		Rare winter migrant, more common autumn
Kumlien's Gull *Larus glaucoides kumlieni*	S	Very rare migrant
Lanceolated Warbler *Locustella lanceolata*	R	Very rare autumn migrant
Lapland Bunting *Calcarius lapponicus*		Fairly rare, mainly autumn migrant
Lapwing *Vanellus vanellus*		Uncommon autumn migrant & winter visitor
Laughing Gull *Larus atricilla*	R	Very rare migrant
Leach's Petrel *Oceanodroma leucorhoa*	S	Rare autumn migrant
Least Sandpiper *Calidris minutilla*	R	Very rare autumn migrant
Lesser Black-backed Gull *Larus fuscus*		Very common breeder and summer visitor. Uncommon migrant
Lesser Crested Tern *Sterna bengalensis*	R	Very rare autumn migrant
Lesser Grey Shrike *Lanius minor*	R	Very rare, mainly autumn migrant
Lesser Kestrel *Falco naumanni*	R	Very rare migrant
Lesser Redpoll *Carduelis cabaret*		Fairly rare, mainly autumn migrant
Lesser Scaup *Aythya affinis*	R	Very rare
Lesser Whitethroat *Sylvia curruca*		Fairly rare, mainly autumn migrant
Lesser Yellowlegs *Tringa flavipes*	R	Very rare, mainly autumn migrant
Linnet *Carduelis cannabina*		Common migrant. Breeds. Fairly common summer visitor. Fairly rare winter visitor

Name		Status & when seen
Little Auk *Alle alle*		Fairly rare, mainly autumn migrant. Rare winter visitor
Little Bittern *Ixobrychus minutus*	R	Very rare spring migrant
Little Bunting *Emberiza pusilla*	S	Rare, mainly autumn migrant
Little Bustard *Tetrax tetrax*	R	Very rare migrant
Little Crake *Porzana parva*	R	Very rare autumn migrant
Little Egret *Egretta garzetta*		Rare resident. Fairly rare winter migrant
Little Grebe *Tachybaptus ruficollis*		Rare winter migrant
Little Gull *Larus minutus*		Rare migrant
Little Owl *Athene noctua*	S	Very rare visitor
Little Ringed Plover *Charadrius dubius*	S	Rare migrant
Little Shearwater *Puffinis assimilis*	R	Very rare migrant
Little Stint *Calidris minuta*		Fairly rare, mainly autumn migrant
Little Swift *Apus affinis*	R	Very rare migrant, all spring records
Little Tern *Sterna albifrons*		Rare, mainly spring migrant
Long-billed Dowitcher *Limnodromus scolopaceus*	R	Very rare autumn migrant & winter visitor
Long-eared Owl *Asio otus*		Rare winter migrant
Long-tailed Duck *Clangula hyemalis*		Rare winter migrant
Long-tailed Skua *Stercorarius longicaudus*	S	Very rare autumn migrant
Long-tailed Tit *Aegithalos caudatus*	S	Very rare, mainly autumn migrant
Magnolia Warbler *Dendroica magnolia*	R	Very rare autumn migrant
Magpie *Pica pica*	S	Very rare migrant
Mallard *Anas platyrhynchos*		Fairly common resident
Manx Shearwater *Puffinus puffinus*		Uncommon summer visitor, breeder and migrant
Marsh Harrier *Circus aeruginosus*		Rare migrant
Marsh Sandpiper *Tringa stagnatalis*	R	Very rare migrant
Marsh Warbler *Acrocephalus palustris*	S	Rare, mainly autumn migrant
Meadow Pipit *Anthus pratensis*		Very common, mainly autumn migrant. Uncommon winter visitor. Rare summer visitor and breeder
Mealy Redpoll *Carduelis flammea*	S	Very rare autumn migrant
Mediterranean Gull *Larus melanocephalus*	S	Rare autumn migrant/Winter visitor
Melodious Warbler *Hippolais polyglotta*	S	Rare, mainly autumn migrant
Merlin *Falco columbarius*		Fairly rare, mainly autumn migrant. Rare winter visitor
Mistle Thrush *Turdus viscivorus*		Fairly rare, mainly autumn migrant. Rare winter visitor
Montagu's Harrier *Circus pygargus*	S	Rare, mainly spring migrant
Moorhen *Gallinula chloropus*		Uncommon resident
Mute Swan *Cygnus olor*		Fairly rare resident
Night Heron *Nycticorax nycticorax*	S	Rare, mainly spring migrant
Nighthawk *Chordeiles minor*	R	Very rare autumn migrant
Nightingale *Luscinia megarhynchos*	S	Very rare migrant
Nightjar *Caprimulgus europaeus*	S	Rare migrant and summer visitor

BIRDS

Birds of Scilly (continued)

Name		Status & when seen
Northern Parula *Parula americana*	R	Very rare autumn migrant
Northern Waterthrush *Seiurus aurocapillus*	R	Very rare autumn migrant
Nutcracker *Nucifraga caryocatactes*	R	Very rare autumn migrant
Olive-backed Pipit *Anthus hodgsonii*	R	Rare autumn migrant
Oriental Turtle Dove *Streptopelia orientalis*	R	Very rare spring migrant
Orphean Warbler *Sylvia hortensis*	R	Very rare autumn migrant
Ortolan Bunting *Emberiza hortulana*	S	Fairly rare, mainly autumn migrant
Osprey *Pandion haliaetus*	S	Rare migrant
Oystercatcher *Haematopus ostralegus*		Fairly common winter migrant. Uncommon summer visitor and breeder
Pacific Golden Plover *Pluvialis fulva*	R	Very rare autumn migrant
Paddyfield Warbler *Acrocephalus agricola*	R	Very rare, mainly autumn migrant
Pale-bellied Brent Goose *Branta bernicla hrota*		Rare winter migrant
Pallas's Warbler *Phylloscopus proregulus*	S	Rare autumn migrant
Pallid Swift *Apus pallidus*	R	Very rare spring migrant, also seen June and October
Pechora Pipit *Anthus gustavi*	R	Very rare autumn migrant
Pectoral Sandpiper *Calidris melanotos*		Rare, mainly autumn migrant
Penduline Tit *Remiz pendulinus*	R	Rare autumn migrant
Peregrine Falcon *Falco peregrinus*		Rare resident and migrant
Pheasant *Phasianus colchicus*		Uncommon resident
Philadelphia Vireo *Vireo philadelphicus*	R	Very rare autumn migrant
Pied Flycatcher *Ficedula hypoleuca*		Fairly common, mainly autumn migrant
Pied Wagtail *Motacilla alba yarellii*		Uncommon, mainly autumn migrant. Rare winter visitor. Very rare summer visitor and breeder
Pied Wheatear *Oenanthe pleschanka*	R	Very rare autumn migrant
Pied-billed Grebe *Podilymbus podiceps*	R	Very rare winter visitor
Pine Bunting *Emberiza leucocephalos*	R	Very rare migrant
Pink-footed Goose *Anser brachyrhynchus*	S	Rare migrant
Pintail *Anas acuta*		Rare winter migrant
Pochard *Aythya ferina*		Fairly rare winter visitor, has bred in recent years
Pomarine Skua *Stercorarius pomarinus*	S	Rare, mainly autumn migrant
Puffin *Fratercula arctica*		Uncommon summer visitor and breeder. Rare autumn migrant
Purple Heron *Ardea purpurea*	S	Rare, mainly spring migrant

Fishing flock of shag

Birds of Scilly (continued)

Name		Status & when seen
Purple Sandpiper *Calidris maritima*		Uncommon, mainly spring migrant. Winter visitor
Quail *Coturnix coturnix*		Rare, mainly spring migrant
Radde's Warbler *Phylloscopus schwarzi*	R	Rare autumn migrant
Raven *Corvus corax*		Rare resident
Razorbill *Alca torda*		Fairly common summer visitor, breeds and winter migrant
Red Kite *Milvus milvus*	S	Very rare, mainly autumn migrant and winter visitor
Red-backed Shrike *Lanius collurio*		Rare, mainly autumn migrant
Red-billed Tropicbird *Phaethon aethereus*	R	Very rare Migrant
Red-breasted Flycatcher *Ficedula parva*		Fairly rare, mainly autumn migrant
Red-breasted Merganser *Mergus serrator*		Rare winter migrant
Red-crested Pochard *Netta rufina*	S	Very rare autumn migrant
Red-eyed Vireo *Vireo olivaceus*	R	Rare autumn migrant
Red-footed Falcon *Falco vespertinus*	R	Very rare spring migrant
Red-legged Partridge *Alectoris rufa*	I	Resident all inhabited islands except St Agnes. Breeds
Red-necked Grebe *Podiceps grisegena*	S	Very rare winter migrant
Red-necked Phalarope *Phalaropus lobatus*	S	Very rare migrant
Red-rumped Swallow *Hirundo daurica*	R	Very rare migrant
Redshank *Tringa totanus*		Uncommon, mainly autumn migrant. Fairly rare winter visitor
Redstart *Phoenicurus phoenicurus*		Uncommon, mainly autumn migrant
Red-throated Diver *Gavia stellata*	S	Rare winter migrant
Red-throated Pipit *Anthus cervinus*	R	Very rare, mainly autumn migrant
Redwing *Turdus iliacus*		Common, mainly autumn migrant. Fairly common winter visitor
Reed Bunting *Emberiza schoeniclus*		Fairly rare migrant
Reed Warbler *Acrocephalus scirpaceus*		Uncommon, mainly autumn migrant. Rare breeder and summer visitor
Richard's Pipit *Anthus novaeseelandiae*	S	Fairly rare, mainly autumn migrant
Ring Ouzel *Turdus torquatus*		Uncommon, mainly autumn migrant
Ring-billed Gull *Larus delawarensis*	S	Rare migrant
Ringed Plover *Charadrius hiaticula*		Fairly common resident. Uncommon winter migrant

BIRDS

Birds of Scilly (continued)

Name		Status & when seen
Ring-necked Duck *Aythya collaris*	S	Very rare autumn migrant
Ring-necked Parakeet *Psittacula krameri*	S	Very rare, recorded Dec 1985
Robin *Erithacus rubecula*		Common resident. Fairly rare, mainly autumn migrant
Rock Pipit *Anthus petrosus*		Common resident
Rock Thrush *Monticola saxatilis*	R	Very rare migrant
Roller *Coracias garrulus*	R	Very rare migrant
Rook *Corvus frugilegus*		Rare, mainly spring migrant
Roseate Tern *Sterna dougallii*	S	Rare migrant, summer visitor and breeder
Rose-breasted Grosbeak *Pheucticus ludovicianis*	R	Very rare autumn migrant
Rose-coloured Starling *Sturnus roseus*	S	Rare autumn migrant, also seen June/July
Rough-legged Buzzard *Buteo lagopus*	S	Very rare migrant
Ruddy Duck *Oxyura jamaicensis*	S	Very rare autumn migrant and winter visitor
Ruff *Philomachus pugnax*		Fairly rare, mainly autumn migrant. Very rare winter visitor
Rustic Bunting *Emberiza rustica*	R	Rare autumn migrant
Sabine's Gull *Larus sabini*	S	Rare autumn migrant
Sand Martin *Riparia riparia*		Fairly common spring migrant, smaller numbers autumn
Sanderling *Calidris alba*		Fairly common winter migrant
Sandwich Tern *Sterna sandvicensis*		Uncommon, mainly autumn migrant
Sardinian Warbler *Sylvia melanocephala*	R	Very rare migrant
Scandinavian Chiffchaff *Phylloscopus c. abietinus*	S	Fairly rare autumn migrant
Scandinavian Rock Pipit *Anthus petrosus littoralis*		Very rare migrant
Scarlet Tanager *Piranga olivacea*	R	Very rare autumn migrant
Scaup *Aythya marila*		Rare winter migrant
Scops Owl *Otus scops*	R	Very rare spring migrant
Sedge Warbler *Acrocephalus schoenabaenus*		Fairly common, mainly autumn migrant. Fairly rare summer visitor and breeder
Semipalmated Plover *Charadrius semipalmatus*	R	Very rare autumn migrant
Semipalmated Sandpiper *Calidris pusilla*	R	Very rare autumn migrant
Serin *Serinus serinus*	S	Rare, mainly autumn migrant
Shag *Phalacrocorax aristotelis*		Very common resident
Sharp-tailed Sandpiper *Calidris acuminata*	R	Very rare autumn migrant
Shelduck *Tadorna tadorna*		Fairly rare summer visitor, breeder and winter visitor
Shore Lark *Eremophila alpestris*	S	Very rare migrant
Short-eared Owl *Asio flammeus*		Rare, mainly autumn migrant
Short-toed Eagle *Circaetus gallicus*	R	Very rare migrant
Short-toed Lark *Calandrella brachydactyla*	S	Rare, mainly autumn migrant
Shoveler *Anas clypeata*		Fairly rare autumn migrant and winter visitor
Siberian Chiffchaff *Phylloscopus c.tristis*	S	Rare autumn migrant and winter visitor
Siberian Thrush *Zoothera sibirica*	R	Very rare autumn migrant
Siskin *Carduelis spinus*		Fairly common, mainly autumn migrant

Name		Status & when seen
Skylark *Alauda arvensis*		Uncommon regular autumn and winter migrant. Not resident since 1999
Slavonian Grebe *Podiceps auritus*	S	Rare winter migrant
Smew *Mergus albellus*		Very rare winter visitor
Regular Snipe *Gallinago gallinago*		Fairly common migrant. Uncommon winter visitor
Snow Bunting *Plectrophenax nivalis*		Fairly rare, mainly autumn migrant
Snowy Owl *Nyctea scandiaca*	R	Very rare winter migrant
Soft-plumaged Petrel sp *Pterodroma madeira/ mollis/feae*	R	Very rare autumn migrant. At least one if not two sightings now accepted as Fea's Petrel
Solitary Sandpiper *Tringa solitaria*	R	Very rare autumn migrant
Song Thrush *Turdus philomelos*		Common resident. Fairly common, mainly autumn migrant and winter visitor
Sooty Shearwater *Puffinis griseus*		Fairly rare autumn migrant
Sora *Porzana carolina*	R	Very rare autumn migrant
Spanish Sparrow *Passer hispaniolensis*	R	Very rare autumn migrant
Spanish Wagtail *Motacilla flava iberiae*	S	Very rare spring migrant
Sparrowhawk *Accipiter nisus*		Rare winter, spring and summer migrant
Spectacled Warbler *Sylvia conspicillata*	R	Very rare autumn migrant
Spoonbill *Platalea leucorodia*		Very rare migrant
Spotted Crake *Porzana porzana*	S	Rare, mainly autumn migrant
Spotted Flycatcher *Muscicapa striata*		Fairly common migrant. Rare summer visitor and breeder
Spotted Redshank *Tringa erythropus*		Rare, mainly autumn migrant
Spotted Sandpiper *Actitis macularia*	R	Very rare, mainly autumn migrant
Squacco Heron *Ardeola ralloides*	R	Very rare spring migrant
Starling *Sturnus vulgaris*		Very common, mainly autumn migrant: Fairly common resident
Stock Dove *Columba oenas*		Uncommon, mainly autumn migrant. Fairly rare winter visitor. Rarely breeds
Stone Curlew *Burhinus oedicnemus*	S	Very rare spring migrant, also seen autumn
Stonechat *Saxicola torquata*		Uncommon resident and migrant
Storm Petrel *Hydrobates pelagicus*		Very common summer visitor and breeds
Subalpine Warbler *Sylvia cantillans*	R	Rare migrant
Surf Scoter *Melanitta perspicillata*	S	Very rare autumn and winter migrant
Swainson's Thrush *Catharus ustulatus*	R	Very rare autumn migrant
Swallow *Hirundo rustica*		Very common migrant. Fairly rare summer visitor and breeder
Swift *Apus apus*		Fairly common migrant
Taiga Bean Goose *Anser fabalis fabalis*	S	Very rare autumn migrant
Tawny Owl *Strix aluco*	S	Very rare winter migrant
Tawny Pipit *Anthus campestris*	S	Rare, mainly autumn migrant
Teal *Anas crecca*		Uncommon winter migrant. Very rare summer visitor and breeder
Temminck's Stint *Calidris temminckii*	S	Very rare migrant

BIRDS

Name		Status & when seen
Terek Sandpiper *Xenus cinereus*	R	Very rare spring migrant
Thrush Nightingale *Luscinia luscinia*	R	Very rare autumn migrant
Tree Pipit *Anthus trivialis*		Uncommon migrant
Tree Sparrow *Passer montanus*	S	Rare migrant
Tree Swallow *Tachycineta bicolor*	R	Very rare
Treecreeper *Certhia familiaris*	S	Very rare autumn migrant
Tufted Duck *Aythya fuligula*		Fairly rare resident. Rare winter migrant
Tundra Bean Goose *Anser fabalis rossicus*	S	Very rare winter visitor
Turnstone *Arenaria interpres*		Fairly common winter migrant
Turtle Dove *Streptopelia turtur*		Uncommon, mainly spring migrant
Twite *Carduelis flavirostris*	S	Very rare autumn migrant
Two-barred Greenish Warbler *Phylloscopus trochiloides plumbeitarsus*	R	Very rare autumn migrant
Upland Sandpiper *Bartramia longicauda*	R	Very rare autumn migrant
Velvet Scoter *Melanitta fusca*	S	Very rare autumn migrant and winter visitor
Water Pipit *Anthus spinoletta*	S	Rare, mainly autumn migrant
Water Rail *Rallus aquaticus*		Uncommon winter migrant
Waxwing *Bombycilla garrulus*	S	Very rare, mainly autumn migrant and winter visitor
Western Black-eared Wheatear *Oenanthe hispanica hispanica*	R	Very rare migrant
Western Bonelli's Warbler *Phylloscopus bonelli*	R	Rare, mainly autumn migrant
Western Sandpiper *Calidris mauri*	R	Very rare autumn migrant
Wheatear *Oenanthe oenanthe*		Fairly common migrant. Very rarely breeds.
Whimbrel *Numenius phaeopus*		Uncommon, mainly spring migrant
Whinchat *Saxicola rubetra*		Uncommon, mainly autumn migrant
White Stork *Ciconia ciconia*	S	Very rare migrant
White Wagtail *Motacilla alba alba*		Uncommon, mainly autumn migrant. Some years almost common spring migrant. Very rarely breeds
White-billed Diver *G. adamsii*	R	Very rare spring migrant
White-rumped Sandpiper *Calidris fuscicollis*	R	Very rare, mainly autumn migrant
White's Thrush *Zoothera dauma*	R	Very rare autumn migrant
White-spotted Bluethroat *Luscinia svecica cyanecula*		Very rare spring migrant
Whitethroat *Sylvia communis*		Uncommon, mainly autumn migrant. Very rare summer visitor and breeder
White-winged Tern *Chlidonias leucopterus*	R	Very rare migrant
Whooper Swan *Cygnus cygnus*		Rare winter migrant
Wigeon *Anas penelope*		Fairly rare winter migrant
Willow Warbler *Phylloscopus trochilus*		Fairly common migrant. Fairly rare summer visitor and breeder
Wilson's Phalarope *Phalaropus tricolor*	R	Very rare autumn migrant
Wilson's Snipe *Gallinago gallinago delicata*	R	Very rare autumn migrant
Wilson's Storm-petrel *Oceanites oceanicus*	R	Rare but now regular early autumn migrant
Wood Sandpiper *Tringa glareola*		Rare, mainly autumn migrant

Name		Status & when seen
Wood Thrush *Hylocichla mustelina*	R	Very rare autumn migrant
Wood Warbler *Phylloscopus sibilatrix*		Fairly rare migrant
Woodchat Shrike *Lanius senator*	S	Rare migrant
Woodcock *Scolopax rusticola*		Uncommon winter migrant
Woodlark *Lullula arborea*	S	Rare autumn migrant
Woodpigeon *Columba palumbus*		Fairly common resident and autumn migrant
Wren *Troglodytes troglodytes*		Very common resident
Wryneck *Jynx torquilla*		Fairly rare, mainly autumn migrant
Yellow Wagtail *Motacilla flava flavissima*		Uncommon migrant
Yellow-bellied Sapsucker *Sphyrapicus varius*	R	Very rare autumn migrant
Yellow-billed Cuckoo *Coccyzus americanus*	R	Very rare autumn migrant
Yellow-breasted Bunting *Emberiza aureola*	R	Very rare autumn migrant
Yellow-browed Bunting *Emberiza chrysophrys*	R	Very rare autumn migrant
Yellow-browed Warbler *Phylloscopus inornatus*		Fairly rare autumn migrant
Yellowhammer *Emberiza citrinella*	S	Rare, mainly autumn migrant
Yellow-legged Gull *Larus argentatus michahellis*	S	Rare winter migrant
Yellow-rumped Warbler *Dendroica coronata*	R	Very rare autumn migrant
Yellowthroat *Goethlypis trichas*	R	Very rare autumn migrant

Peregrine

BIRDS

Mammals

Grey Seals

Big game on the Isles of Scilly means Grey Atlantic Seal. And they do not come much bigger or meaner than a large bull. The largest predatory mammal in Britain, a bull seal can reach over two metres in length and weigh more than 200 kg. On land their lumbering, quivering bulk and Roman nose profile look impressive, and underwater they are formidable creatures that can move amazingly fast. As the breeding season approaches they divide into male and female groups.

A bull seal will defend his territory, a stretch of coast or a small island, with considerable force. Fights are common in late summer as the breeding season for seals gets into gear. Any cow seals that come ashore to give birth will be mated by the resident bull before they finally return to sea. August finds the cows heavy with young, for here the pups are born before summer ends. This colony is among the earliest to breed in the British Isles. They give birth to a single pup somewhere above the high-water mark on a rocky shore. Delivery is fast, aided by the animal's streamlined shape. From the first signs of labour to the moment of birth may be no more than 15 minutes.

At birth the pups are covered in a dense creamy fur and their skin is loose, hanging in folds. Seal milk is among the richest in the animal world. Suckled every five or six hours, the youngsters rapidly gain weight. Within a few weeks they can treble their birth weight, and only then will their mothers leave them, usually after about 21 days. Left alone, the bloated pups begin to moult into their short, grey adult fur, but it is a race against time before the first autumn gales sweep across the islands.

The cows are ready to desert their young at the first hint of danger. However, the pups are not as helpless as they appear. To humans, their large black eyes and pale fur make them attractive, but it is an unwise person who attempts to touch a seal pup. Not only is it possible that human scent will cause the cow to desert her young, but the pup has a full set of sharp adult teeth within days of being born. Its milk teeth are produced and reabsorbed while still inside the womb.

The seal pup's routine is a simple one, divided between eating and sleeping, and after three weeks, instead of its appealing good looks, it takes on the appearance of an overweight furry barrel of fat. Maternal care among seals is short-lived, and the cows now leave their pups to fend for themselves.

Meanwhile, the bulls, who play no part in the pups' upbringing, wait offshore to catch the cows. Mating is now or never, as the cows are receptive only at this time. Gestation lasts about nine months, so how do seals give birth at the same time each year? The answer is in the fertilised egg. Starting around fifteen days after the previous birth, the embryo grows slowly for ten days. Then, almost unbelievably, it stops. For 100 days, development is suspended. Then the embryo begins its normal growth for the remaining 240 days. Altogether, this gestation time adds up to one year. It is a vital adaptation, which enables seals to have the freedom of the seas.

Meanwhile, the pup is left on its own, and moves inland as if reluctant to go to sea.

Grey Seal

Although they can swim from birth, the pups need to moult. White fur is rubbed off on rocks, or floats in rock pools stagnant with the verdant bloom of summer algae. On warm days, or when excited, seals weep profusely, for unlike ourselves and other land mammals they lack tear ducts to drain away the fluid. By now the pup's mother will be far away, perhaps feeding for the first time in weeks. For a time the pup lives off the fat gained from its mother's milk, until eventually hunger drives it down to the water's edge.

Grey seal mainly feed on bottom-living fish. They can dive to over 100 metres and can remain submerged for up to 20 minutes. Reports of seals feeding reveal that many other species of small fish may benefit from their activity. They will lift surprisingly large rocks on the sea-bed to find food hidden underneath.

They spend most of their time at sea, but being inquisitive they will readily come close to humans in the water. They are more nervous when on land. At low tide they haul themselves onto exposed rocks for a quick siesta or a spot of sunbathing. They seem impressively at home in the roughest of seas.

Summer brings calmer weather and the opportunity to see them at close quarters from a boat. Up to 300 live around Scilly (over half the world's populations), forming the most southerly breeding colony in Britain. Every year around 80 pups are born in late summer and some years can still be found well into autumn, and despite the high number of pups which seem to die every year from natural causes, the island population of these magnificent creatures appears to be relatively static in recent decades. Many are resident but others migrate around the British coast, as well as across to the Channel Islands and France.

The Western Rocks form their principal breeding grounds, while the more sheltered Eastern Isles are favoured for hauling out and sunbathing. Here they can be found sleeping while floating upright in the water, anchored by a flipper to some Thongweed.

They are unable to give birth at sea, and so are forced to find suitable sites where they can safely produce their pups each year. The Isles of Scilly offer many such places. Bull seals are bigger than cows, and are easily distinguished by their heavy Roman-nosed muzzles.

Seals are quite capable of moving over land, but progress is slow and undignified as they drag their quivering bulk across the rocks; front flippers, more suited to sliding easily through water, make ungainly legs. Their sparse mottled fur helps to protect their skin from abrasion.

Underwater, they are different animals. In the subdued blue world of waving weeds, they slip effortlessly in and out of sight, their curving bodies twisting and turning gracefully. The cumbersome animal that heaved itself across land now torpedoes along with amazing speed. The fur serves a different purpose here, keeping a permanent layer of water close to the skin. In the same way as a wetsuit keeps a diver warm, the seal's warm water layer helps to reduce its heat loss. But the seal's real solution to the problem of insulation is its blubber, a thick layer of oily fat just under the skin that wraps the body in a highly efficient thermal coat.

Summer is the best time to go seal-watching by boat. The island skippers always seem to know where to find good numbers hauled out on their favourite rocks. Just how a large seal clambers to the top of a steep granite slab often puzzles visitors. The answer is simple. The seals float onto the summit at high tide and wait for the water to drop! When the tide returns they simply slip into the sea and resume fishing.

Grey Seal pup

TIPS FOR SEAL-WATCHING

Early in the year they are more curious and will allow a closer approach, but by late summer they are bored by boats.

Watch quietly from a distance; from a boat is best.

On land take care not to approach pups too closely or the mother may not come back. Pups may miss vital feeds or even be abandoned.

Pups may look helpless or appear abandoned, but the mother is usually in the sea not far away, watching her young and you.

Do not attempt to handle pups or adult seals – they have big teeth and will use them!

Bull Grey Seal

Dolphin family between Tresco and St Mary's

Dolphins, Porpoises and Whales

These marine mammals all belong to a group of creatures known as cetaceans. Many are sighted around the islands every year, and recent research using underwater microphones indicates that those seen on the surface are just a tiny proportion of the amazing numbers that seem to be offshore.

Schools of Common Dolphin are often reported, not infrequently between the islands. Harbour Porpoise and Risso's Dolphin can sometimes be seen in good numbers, but more usually they stay in small family groups.

The remains of some larger cetaceans are also occasionally washed ashore. Bottled-nosed Dolphin, Killer Whale, Long-finned Pilot Whale and more rarely Sperm Whale have all been found in Scilly. Most of the bones washed up seem to find their way into island gardens.

Land Mammals

Considering their isolation, the lack of variety of mammals in Scilly is hardly surprising. The resident land mammals that currently live in Scilly have all probably been introduced at some time in the past.

RABBITS

Rabbits are common in Scilly as elsewhere in the rest of Britain. It is thought they were introduced in Norman times as a valuable source of fur and fresh meat, or perhaps long before. Their burrows and scattered excavations riddle many parts of the main islands and also some of the smaller eastern isles. In the past they thrived in the absence of ground-living predators, for the islands have no Foxes, Badgers, Stoats or Weasels, and Buzzards are rare, making them safe from air attack. But the outbreak of myxomatosis in the islands has now greatly reduced the Rabbit population. The fragile ecology of an island is easily ruined by thoughtless introductions and with the decline of rabbits there has been a change in the flora.

HEDGEHOGS

Hedgehogs are another possible threat to the islands' wildlife which have been thoughtlessly released in recent times. They appear harmless but are actually carnivorous, feasting on insects, snails and worms. They are also known occasionally to take small birds' eggs and chicks. Hedgehogs explore sand dunes and beaches in their amblings and so could represent a risk to ground-nesting Ringed Plovers and Terns. They could also compete with a smaller, more famous, cousin.

SCILLY SHREW

Closely related to the Hedgehog, but very different in character and size, there is only one type of shrew in the islands – the Lesser White-toothed Shrew, which is quite unlike the native red-toothed British mainland shrew. The Scilly Shrew is continental in origin and very similar to those found on Jersey, Sark and in France. It is distinguished by its clean teeth. Scilly shrews were first reported in Victorian times and it is possible that they were yet another stowaway on boats that traded in the past with France and the Channel Islands. They can be found almost everywhere in hedgerows and banks, under bracken and especially along the boulder-strewn shores.

Life is short for a shrew, probably not more than a year or two in the wild, and the pace of life they lead appears breathless to us. An hour or so of frantic activity, finding food, eating, cleaning, investigating, shrieking and socialising, is followed by a similar period of rest, throughout the day and night.

For such tiny creatures, their appetites are huge. They must consume almost their own body weight every day just to stay alive, and beetles, fly larvae and Sand Hoppers are eagerly demolished with their sharp little teeth. The shrew's face and tail bristle with stiff sensory hairs and these, together with its long, pointed, ever-twitching nose, signal the importance of touch and smell in its life.

Shrews live life in the fast lane. Even their rate of reproduction is high. Three to four litters can be produced every year, each containing up to six young. Born blind and naked, the young quickly develop a thin coat of hair at around nine days old and their eyes open soon after. It is from about this age that a curious form of behaviour known as caravanning may on rare occasions be witnessed. It is an extraordinary scene to watch and one for which the Scilly Shrew is justifiably famous. In what seems to be a response to a threat or disturbance to the nest, the female shrew dives inside and quickly reappears with her offspring, literally, in tow. The young, holding on by their teeth, are led to safety. Sometimes they all cling on together, gripping the skin on their mother's back, half dragged, half carried. More entertainingly, the young bite hold at the base of each other's tail. The result is a train of shrews with their mother in the lead and the rest of the family trailing behind.

Shrew caravan

The tables below record mammals found in the islands – residents, visitors and the remains of sea mammals washed ashore. Perhaps the most amazing is the polar bear!

Land mammals

Name	Notes
Common Rat *Rattus norvegicus*	Accidentally introduced from ships
Hedgehog *Erinaceus europaeus*	Introduced
House Mouse *Mus domesticus*	Found in all inhabited islands
Lesser White-toothed or Scilly Shrew *Crocidura suaveolens cassiteridium*	Probable accidental introduction, perhaps as early as the Bronze Age. Found on all inhabited islands as well as Annet and Samson.
Polar Bear *Ursus maritimus*	Possible carcass seen floating in St Mary's Sound in 1966!
Rabbit *Oryctolagus cuniculus*	Found on many islands before 1176.
Wood Mouse *Apodemus sylvaticus*	Probably accidentally introduced to St Mary's and Tresco by early settlers

Bats

Brandt's Bat *Myotis brandti*	Possible identification from bat detector
Brown Long-eared Bat *Plecotus auritus*	Last recorded in the mid-1960s
Noctule *Nyctalus noctula*	Migrant
Pipistrelle *Pipistrellus pipistrellus*	Resident
Whiskered Bat *Myotis mystacinus*	Possible identification from bat detector

Marine mammals

Atlantic Grey Seal *Halichoerus grypus*	Resident colony
Blue Whale *Balaenoptera musculus*	Stranding in 1843
Bottle-nosed Dolphin *Tursiops truncatus*	Regular visitor
Common Dolphin *Delphinus delphis*	Often seen offshore, especially from *The Scillonian*
Cuvier's Beaked Whale *Ziphius cavirostris*	Occasional visitor
False Killer Whale *Pseudorca crassidens*	Stranding in 1974
Fin Whale *Balaenoptera physalis*	A few recent records since 1996
Humpback Whale *Megaptera novaeangliae*	Occasional visitor
Killer Whale (Orca) *Orcinus orca*	Occasional visitor
Long-finned Pilot Whale *Globicephala melas*	Occasional visitor
Minke Whale *Balaenoptera acutorostrata*	Occasional visitor
Northern Right Whale *Eubalena glacialis*	Reduced numbers in recent years
Porpoise *Phocoena phocoena*	Infrequent visitor around the islands
Risso's or Grey Dolphin *Grampus griseus*	Occasionally recorded offshore
Sei Whale *Balaenoptera borealis*	One live stranding
Sowerby's Beaked Whale *Mesoplodon bidens*	Three strandings, the last one in 1991
Sperm Whale *Physeter catodon*	Occasional visitor
Striped Dolphin *Stenella coeruleoalba*	Occasional visitor
White-beaked Dolphin *Lagenorhynchus albirostris*	Occasional visitor
White-sided Dolphin *Lagenorhynchus acutus*	Occasional visitor

Reptiles and Amphibians

Thirteen different reptiles and amphibians can be found in the British Isles, yet only the Common Frog seems to be a long-time resident in Scilly. There is evidence of the remains of toad bones from the Bronze Age and a smattering of more recent records of toad sightings from St Mary's and St Agnes, but they may simply be introduced animals or a case of mistaken identity.

The occasional report of a Slow Worm suggests that some may have escaped from captivity or been let loose at some time in the past. Palmate Newt have also been recorded since the 1960s. There are no snakes or other amphibians in Scilly, but sightings of much larger reptiles are not unknown.

Turtles occasionally visit the islands. The most common and biggest by far is the Leatherback Turtle. They have been recorded several times over the last century. They feed extensively on jellyfish and follow their swarms across the Atlantic. While records usually refer to turtles being washed ashore, there are many more reports of these gentle giants from boatmen in the surrounding waters. Less commonly sighted are the Loggerhead, and there is a single record of a Kemp's Ridley Turtle in 1925.

Common Frog

Insects

Many visitors to the islands will have heard of the St Martin's Ant and Scilly Bee, but there are many more related creatures in Scilly.

Stick Insects

Some time in the 1960s a gardener in the Abbey Gardens was at the top of a ladder, cutting a particularly tall hedge. Suddenly he was startled by a huge insect landing on him and lost his balance. Luckily he survived the fall with only a broken arm, but subsequent searches revealed a thriving population of giant living twigs – stick insects. These inoffensive, plant-eating creatures must have arrived unnoticed on some imported plants. Two different species were discovered – the **Smooth** and the **Prickly**. More recently a third one has been added to the list – the **Mediterranean or Corsican Stick Insect**. Most stick insects are small, but some can grow almost as long as a human's forearm, so no wonder the poor gardener was frightened. The Smooth and Prickly Stick Insects are native to New Zealand. One of them must have survived the long journey from its home hidden amongst some foliage, and one female is all that is needed to start a colony. Remarkably, female stick insects can breed without a mate. They lay eggs that all hatch as females.

Other insects also thrive in the gardens. Bees and beneficial Hover Flies are attracted to flowers that produce a rich flow of nectar. Giant Echiums from the cloud forests of the Canaries attract large numbers of bees in early summer. Better still is the flamboyant Metrosideros tree, which is one of the richest sources of nectar in the Abbey Gardens. Their brilliant red flowers are borne high in the canopy and on warm days they buzz with life.

Ants

Out of the 36 different species of ants recorded in Britain, 13 have been recorded in Scilly and only 10 are currently found. The most intriguing is the so-called **St Martin's or Red-barbed Ant**, *Formica rufibarbis*, a real rarity. First discovered in Britain in 1896, they were recorded from six mainland sites on Surrey heathlands and one in the Scilly Isles, on Chapel Down at the east end of St Martin's. Today they are restricted to just two sites in Surrey living in just a handful of colonies, while the outpost in Scilly is still thought to be present; they were last reported on St Martin's in 1997.

Elsewhere this ant is found in southern and central Europe. They are one of the most warmth-loving ants of their kind, living in open areas of short, lowland grass or heather. The nests are excavated in the ground or under stones that readily warm up in the sun. Each nest may contain a colony of a few thousand workers along with one or more queens and their brood. The workers forage alone for invertebrate prey to feed their growing youngsters and will also take nectar and aphid honeydew.

Smooth Stick Insect

Healthy colonies produce new winged queens and males every year and mating flights most commonly occur in July. Caught in updrafts or thermals, they may be carried far by strong winds. It was probably in this way that this ant came to the islands many centuries or even millennia ago, perhaps long before people arrived in Scilly. In the world of these industrious little workers it takes just one fertilised queen to establish a dynasty.

Please replace any stones moved, if you are looking for ants.

Ants of Scilly

Name	Most active	Status and where found
Common Elbowed Red Ant *Myrmica scabrinodis*	April-Sept	Most common of its kind, on all inhabited islands, coast and inland, under stones
Red Ant *Myrmica ruginodis*	April-Sept	Common, recorded on all inhabited islands, coast and inland, under stones
Red Ant *Myrmica sabuleti*	April-Sept	Less common than two above, on all inhabited islands except Bryher, coast and inland, under stones
Turf Ant *Tetramorium caespitum*	April-Sept	Inconspicuous, smaller than the above, on all inhabited islands except Bryher, coast and inland, under stones
Negro Ant *Formica fusca*	April-Sept	Common and widespread on all inhabited islands except St Agnes, often seen foraging on white umbellifer flowers
St Martin's Ant *Formica rufibarbis*	April-Sept	Rare, restricted to the east end of Chapel Down, St Martin's. Has also been found on Eastern Isles and Tean. Nests under stones
Small Black Ant *Lasius niger*	April-Sept	Common and conspicuous, all inhabited islands, in gardens and coast under stones
Sand-loving ant *Lasius psammophillius*	April-Sept	Frequent coastal heathland and dunes, all inhabited islands, under stones and heather tussocks.
Common Yellow Ant *Lasius flavus*	April-Sept	Common all inhabited islands, grassland, coastal heath and sandy areas
Jet Ant *Lasius fuliginosus*	April-Sept	Discovered 2002, Pelistry, St Mary's.

ANTS

St Martin's Ant

Bees

The soft sandy strata of some of the islands' low cliffs offer ideal excavation sites for a harmless little bee to dig its nest. These *Andrena* mining bees belong to a large and successful group of solitary bees containing some 60 different species. They cannot harm people, as their sting is so weak it is unable to penetrate human skin. Several mining bees are found in Scilly, but one is a special island race. Small and dark-coloured, the female alone digs a tiny tunnel, making perhaps six or more earthen chambers in which to lay her eggs. There is no parental care. She shows no interest in the burrow after completing its construction and stocking it with provisions for her brood. Although solitary, the individual nests are often so closely packed together that they appear to be a thriving colony, yet each one maintains a separate life. Despite being relatively common in Scilly this mining bee is another mainland rarity.

Unlike mining bees, bumblebees are sociable and live in colonies. They are not as aggressive as wasps and hornets, and differ from honey bees in that they do not die when they sting. Bumblebees have a smooth, unbarbed stinger but are relatively docile creatures which pose no threat to people.

Bumblebees are widespread, but not all are common and some are very rare. Britain has over 25 different species, only nine of which have been recorded in Scilly. Their worker bees die over winter and so the queen must start a new colony each year. Even the largest nests seldom contain more than 400 individuals and often considerably less.

One bee is rather special. The **Moss Carder Bee** is small and seems to thrive in damp conditions around the British Isles. It builds its home in marsh and coastal areas, often above ground and deep in moss. They generally have attractive, orange-brown and yellow colouring but the one in Scilly is no ordinary bee. Here in Scilly it is a distinct subspecies, an island race similar to one found on Alderney in the Channel Islands. Once widespread in Scilly, their numbers have sadly dwindled in recent years. Today St Agnes seems to be their last stronghold. Their decline is perhaps caused by the loss of flower-rich grasslands due to the lack of grazing and the subsequent invasion of bracken. When working on my first BBC programme in the islands in 1980, I found that this particular bee was only known to science. It seemed obvious to give *Bombus muscorum scyllonius* a common name, so I did – the **Scilly Bee**.

The following tables only include those which are special to the islands or can be most commonly found. Two dates indicate two broods a year.

Do not disturb nests of social wasps and bees, some can be very aggressive in defence of their home. (Information after I. C. Beavis.)

Bumblebee on Hottentot Fig　　　　　　　*Overleaf: Scilly Bee on Three-cornered Leek*

Bees and Wasps of Scilly

Name	Most active	Notes
BEES		
Honey Bee *Apis mellifera*	April-Sept	Most managed in apiaries. Because of a parasitic mite few colonies now survive long in wild. Found on all the inhabited islands, from gardens to heathland
Colletes similis	June-Sept	Common on all inhabited islands especially July-August on Sea Mayweed, coastal grassland and heathlands
Girdled Colletes *Colletes succintus*	Late July-Aug	Local on heather, on all inhabited islands, scarce on St Agnes and Bryher
Mining Bee *Andrena angustior*	April-July	Common inland and coast, especially in the Abbey Gardens, Tresco
Mining Bee *Andrena nigroaenea sarnia* (island subspecies with orange-brown hairs on thorax and pollen-baskets)	April-June	Common and widespread on all inhabited islands, especially April-May. Often large aggregations, soft cliffs, backs of shores, earth in walls
Mining Bee *Andrena thoracica*	April-early June July-Aug	Common and widespread on all inhabited islands. Often large aggregations shared with *A. nigroaenea*, soft cliffs, backs of shores, earth in walls
Mining bee *Andrena fuscipes*	Late July-Aug	Local on heather, all inhabited islands, most common on St, Mary's and St Martin's
Yellow-legged Mining Bee *Andrena flavipes*	April, May & July	Recent colonist now well established around St Mary's coast in soft cliff and vertical patches of bare earth. Also found on Tresco and St Martin's
Slender Mining Bee *Lasioglossum calceatum*	April-Sept	Common and widespread on all inhabited islands, inland and sheltered coast on Daisy, Ragwort and Bramble
Shaggy Mining Bee *Lasioglossum villosulum*	May-Aug	Common and widespread on all inhabited islands, open grassland and coastal heath. Nests in bare vertical earth on coast and inland
Mining Bee *Lasioglossum smeathmanellum*	April-Aug	Fairly common and widespread on St Mary's, uncommon on other islands. In sheltered coastal areas often seen on sunlit rocks, walls etc.
Cuckoo Bee *Sphecodes monilicornis*	April-July	Common and widespread on all inhabited islands, open grassland and coastal heath
Cuckoo Bee *Sphecodes ephippius*	April-Aug	Common and widespread on all inhabited islands, coast and inland
Cuckoo Bee *Sphecodes geoffrellus*	April-July	Common and widespread on all inhabited islands, inland and coast, smaller than above species

Heather in bloom – good foraging for bees

Bees and Wasps of Scilly (continued)

Name	Most active	Notes
Patchwork Leaf-cutter Bee *Megachile centuncularis*	May-Aug	Common mainland species only recently established in Scilly. Cuts rose leaves. Inland and coastal St Mary's, Tresco and Bryher
Willughby's Leaf-cutter Bee *Megachile willughbiella*	June-Aug	Widespread but not common, only leaf-cutter bee native to Scilly, open grass, heath and gardens. Nests in bare vertical ground
Golden-rod Nomad Bee *Nomada rufipes*	August	Local to coastal heath, widespread but most common on St Mary's and St Martin's. Another so-called cuckoo bee, parasitising nests of *Andrena fuscipes*

BUMBLEBEE

Buff-tailed Bumblebee *Bombus terrestris*	May-Sept some all year	Common and widespread, on all inhabited islands
Red-tailed Bumblebee *Bombus lapidarus*	mid May-Sept	Widespread, mainly coastal grasslands, on all inhabited islands
Early Bumblebee *Bombus pratorum*	April-Aug	Recent colonist, a common mainland bee. Found on Tresco and St Mary's
Small Garden Bumblebee *Bombus hortorum*	May-Sept	Widespread but not common, on all inhabited islands, most frequent on St Mary's
Heath Bumblebee *Bombus jonellus*	July-August	Scarce and declining, now only St Mary's, coastal heath on heather
Scilly Bee *Bombus muscorum scyllonius*	May-Sept	Scarce and declining, its last stronghold on St Agnes, coastal heath and grassland, often on heather and Bird's-foot Trefoil

WASPS

Spider-hunting Wasp *Arachnospila anceps*	May-Aug	Common and widespread. Found on all inhabited islands, coastal heath, grassland and dunes
Mason Wasp *Ancistrocerus gazella*	May-Sept	Recorded on all inhabited islands except St Martin's, sheltered inland areas alongside footpaths etc. Peak numbers in July
Slender Digger Wasp *Crossocerus elongatulus*	April-Sept	Common and widespread. Found on all inhabited islands, sheltered inland and sometimes open grass and heath
Ruby-tailed Wasp *Chrysis rutiliventris*	May-Aug	Common and widespread on all inhabited islands. Parasitises Mason wasp nests
Common Wasp *Vespula vulgaris*	April-Oct	Individual workers recently recorded on Tresco and queens on St Mary's
German Wasp *Vespula germanica*	April-Oct	Individual queens recorded in 1996 on St Mary's and Tresco
Tree Wasp *Dolichovespula sylvestris*	April-Oct	Recorded on all inhabited islands, most common on St Mary's and St Martin's

BEES & WASPS

Butterflies

Despite the apparent frail beauty of their wings, many butterflies are surprisingly strong fliers and travel considerable distances, while others never seem to stray far. There are currently 59 species of butterfly on the British list, and a further ten that occasionally stray across our shores. So perhaps it is not surprising that 23 different butterflies have so far been recorded in Scilly, yet only 11 are counted as resident. **Peacock, Small Tortoiseshell** and **Small White Butterflies** are all strong flyers and highly mobile. Not only can they regularly be seen moving between the islands, but also to and from the mainland. Watching a passing butterfly from the deck of *The Scillonian* is always an amazing experience.

Some butterflies probably have a flourishing core population on the larger islands, surrounded by smaller satellite colonies that may occasionally die out before being repopulated again. Others are more recent arrivals. The **Comma** is a well-known wanderer and has probably only colonised the islands in the last 80 years as their range expanded in southern England. The **Holly Blue** is much newer to island life and was not recorded in Scilly until 1977.

Small populations of sedentary, weak-flying butterflies are most at risk from local extinctions. The **Common Blue** and **Green-veined White** seldom fly far and are therefore vulnerable to storms or fires. In 1938 two eminent entomologists, Ford and Dowdeswell, suggested that even the small 300-metre gap between the islands of Tean and St Martin's could prevent the resident populations from interbreeding. They suggested that the **Tean Blue** was a distinct island population.

The annual movement of butterflies from southern Europe in late spring and the return journey south, brings a bevy of

Painted Lady butterfly   *Monarch butterfly*

BUTTERFLIES

bright wings to the islands every year. Early and late summer is the best time to see migrant butterflies passing through. In some years large numbers of **Clouded Yellow** and **Painted Lady** appear with occasional **Red Admiral**. Rarer still are the really long distance travellers. The magnificent migrating **Monarch** sometimes puts in a guest appearance from the Canary Islands or even North America.

One of the most common butterflies in late summer is the **Small Copper**, which also has a blue-spotted form that can be seen in small numbers. Other butterflies are unique to the islands. The **Meadow Brown** in Scilly seems more brightly coloured than its mainland brethren and is now recognised as a separate subspecies similar to the Irish form. As a species they are common and widespread throughout the archipelago and can sometimes be found in surprisingly large numbers on the smallest islands. So what makes these butterflies distinct? Colour and size are the main considerations, but it is the distribution and pattern of black spots on the underside of the wing that are the markers that measure island races. Not only do these seem to differ from the mainland but they also differ between islands. Even more remarkable was the finding that on the tiny island of Tean there appears to be three distinct populations of Meadow Brown, each group living on three separate hills, just a stone's throw apart.

The **Speckled Wood** is a more recent resident, first noticed in 1903, but it is now also recognised as a separate subspecies. On the mainland this butterfly has yellow markings on the wing, while here in Scilly they appear orange. Their habit also differs. Normally a creature of the woodland edge, here in Scilly they seem to favour isolated trees or hedgerows.

In the table on the next page, the following status scale is used: rare – scarce – uncommon – not common – locally common – fairly common – frequent – common – very common. Regular Scilly species are shown in blue.

Speckled Wood butterfly

Butterflies of Scilly

Name	When flying	Status, caterpillar food plants (in italic)
Whites & Yellows		
Green-veined White *Pieris napi*	Apr-Sept	Possibly resident, sporadic records. Wood, lane, damp meadow, garden. *Garlic Mustard and crucifers*
Large White *Pieris brassicae*	April-Oct	Resident and migrant, common. Wood, farm, garden. *Cabbage and Nasturtium*
Small White *Pieris rapae*	April-Sept	Resident and migrant, common. *Cabbage and most crucifers*
Bath White *Pontia daplidice*	July/Aug	Very rare migrant, seen on St Mary's 1977. *Mignonette*
Brimstone *Genepteryx rhamni*	Mar-Sept	Very rare migrant. Usually on chalklands. recorded 1911. *Buckthorn*
Clouded Yellow *Colias crocea*	April-Oct	Almost annual migrant. *Clover, Vetches and Lucerne*
Pale Clouded Yellow *Colias hyale*	May-Sept	Variable rare migrant. Farm, clover fields. *Lucerne*
Orange Tip *Anthocharis cardamines*	April-June	Rare migrant. Lane, wood edge, recorded on St Mary's in 1986. *Garlic mustard and Cuckoo Flower.*
Milk-weed		
Monarch *Danaus plexippus*	July-Oct	Occasional summer vagrant from North America or Canary Islands. Anywhere, non-breeder.
Admirals, Fritillaries & Vanessids		
Comma *Polygonia c-album*	April-Oct	Not very common, possibly now resident. Wood, hedge, orchard. First recorded in 1971 and returned to Scilly in 2003. *Stinging nettle*
Painted Lady *Vanessa cardui*	May-Oct	Regular migrant, may also breed. Anywhere. *Thistle*
Peacock *Inachis ío*	April-May or July-Sept	Common, resident. Garden, farm, wood, park. *Thistle, Stinging nettle*
Red Admiral *Vanessa atalanta*	April-Nov	Regular migrant, may also breed. Anywhere. *Stinging nettle*
Small Tortoiseshell *Aglais urticae*	Mar-Oct	Fairly common, resident – anywhere, on *Stinging nettle*
Browns		
Meadow Brown *Maniola jurtina cassiteridium*	June-Oct	Common, resident. Grassland everywhere. *Coarse grasses.*
Speckled Wood *Pararge aegeria insula*	April-Oct	Fairly common, resident. Wood rides and edge. *Coarse grasses*
Wall Brown *Lasiomnata megera*	May-Oct	Occasional, resident. Grass banks, cliff, lane, hedge. *Coarse grasses*
Small Heath *Coenonympha pamphilus*	May-Oct	Rare migrant. Down. *Rough grass*
Blues & Coppers		
Common Blue *Polyommatus icarus*	May-Oct	Locally common, resident. Downs, rough grass. *Bird's-foot Trefoil, Clover*
Holly Blue *Celastrina argiolus*	Mar-Oct	Fairly common, resident. First recorded 1971. Wood, garden. *Gorse, Ivy and possibly Hebe*
Small Copper *Lycaena phlaeas*	April-Oct	Common, resident. Grass, down, heathland. *Sorrel, Dock*
Camberwell Beauty	April or July-Aug	Rare vagrant. Central European and North American migrant

Moths

Surprisingly colourful and remarkably varied, most moths are creatures of the night, although many also fly by day. Unlike butterflies, the majority of moths fold their wings flat over their back and their variety of shape and size is far greater than their better-known kin. They range from giant Hawkmoths and splendid **Garden Tiger Moths** to some so small they can only be appreciated under a magnifying glass.

Around 2,500 different moths are known in the British Isles. Many moths annually migrate long distances from the Mediterranean and North Africa, and others even further. So a reasonable number may be expected in Scilly. Moths are broadly divided into two groups, the larger Macro moths and the smaller Micro moths, sometimes described as the 'outdoor clothes variety'. Considering the remoteness of Scilly the actual number of moths discovered on the islands is high – over 500 different species recorded so far.

Moth caterpillars, like butterflies, depend on a wide variety of plants for food. Almost every native and many cultivars of fern, flower, shrub and tree can be food for hungry moth caterpillars. Many adult moths are migrants from the Cornish mainland or France, but finding no suitable food or surroundings in Scilly, they simply carry on their way. Every year the islands enjoy an influx of migrating birds. Yet, almost unseen, the same wind that bring the birds also brings countless numbers of moths. Some of the most exotic varieties include **Old World Webworm, Porter's Rustic, Delicate and Gem.**

One of the most delightful and visible is the day flying **Hummingbird Hawkmoth.** Arriving from the Mediterranean during summer, they can be found hovering and feeding from Red Valerian and many others flowers of the season. Other day flying moths common in the islands include the striking black and red coloured **Six-spot Burnet** and the **Cinnabar.**

Three nationally rare moths can be found on the islands. One of them is severely limited to where its food plant grows. Because the nationally rare Balm-leaved Figwort commonly grows throughout the islands, it is not surprising that the moth, *Nothris congressariella* whose caterpillars feed on its leaves, is also found here.

The relatively mild climate in Scilly encourages some moths, such as the **Light Emerald** and **Willow Beauty** to produce more broods each year than in colder, northern parts of Britain. Another moth, the **L-album Wainscot**, does not even normally survive winter on the British mainland, yet annually produces up to two broods in Scilly. The **Yellow V Moth** is barely a centimetre long and generally inhabits warm temperate regions. In Britain it seems confined to warehouses and cellars feeding on the fungi and wine bottle corks. In Scilly this moth has been recorded in the open on the four largest inhabited islands feeding on old grass cuttings and under the bark of Pittosporum.

Some moths in the islands also have special colour forms. The **Feathered Ranunculus** and **Shuttle-shaped Dart** moths are both darker and prettier than their mainland relatives. Many of the resident **Lesser Yellow Underwing** moths also have stronger cross-line markings on their wings.

Sometimes moth caterpillars are easier to see than the adults. **Grass Eggar** cater-

Cinnabar Moth

pillars are covered in short brown hair and can sometimes be so abundant it is difficult to find a track between them. Longer-haired and black, the 'woolly bear' caterpillar of Garden Tiger moths can also be found in large numbers. While the hairs can irritate human skin, they are eagerly sought by the Cuckoo.

Hummingbird Hawkmoth

Moths of Scilly

Day-flying moths		Most commonly seen & comments
Cinnabar *Tyria jacobaeae*	May-Jul	Very Common Resident in grassy areas, caterpillar found on ragwort.
Feathered Ranunculus *Polymixis lichenea lichenea*	Sep-Nov	This island sub-species can be found roosting in cracks in walls
Hummingbird Hawkmoth *Macroglossum stellatarum*	May-Oct	Regular Migrant often seen feeding on Valerian
Red Underwing *Catocala nupta*	Aug-Oct	Common resident, often found roosting high on walls.
Red-necked Footman *Atolmis rubricollis*	Jun-Jul	Common, on sunny days large swarms found flying above pine belts.
Six-spot Burnet *Zygaena filipendulae stephensi*	Jun-Jul	Very Common Resident, flying or at rest in grassy areas on warm days.
Magpie *Abraxas grossulariata*	Jun-Jul	Common, often seen flying, especially Lower Moors.
Vestal *Rhodometra sacraria*	Sep-Oct	migrant often flushed from grassy areas during times of migration.

MOTHS

Dragonflies and Damselflies

Relatively few of these beautiful insects live on the islands. This is hardly surprising considering the lack of freshwater streams and pools, as well as salt-laden winds. Tresco Great Pool and Lower Moors on St Mary's are probably the best places to watch out for them. Of the 39 species of dragonfly and damselfly resident in Britain, just two are resident on the Isles of Scilly. Only a few can be considered to be commonly seen, while 13 have so far been recorded as visitors.

Dragonflies and Damselflies most commonly seen in Scilly

DAMSELFLIES	When flying	Island status & where found
Blue-tailed Damselfly *Ischnura elegans*	early May-mid Sept	Common resident, St Mary's, Tresco, St Martin's & St Agnes
Common blue Damselfly *Enallagma cyathigerum*	mid May-Sept	Last seen St Mary's 2004
Beautiful Demoiselle *Calopteryx virgo*	early May-early Sept	One seen Gugh 2003
DRAGONFLIES		
Black-tailed Skimmer *Orthetrum cancellatum*	end May-mid Aug	Vagrant, St Mary's 2003
Common Darter *Sympetrum striolatum*	early June-late Oct	Common, resident St Mary's, Tresco, St Martin's & St Agnes
Common Hawker *Aeshna juncea*	early July-early Oct	Found on Tresco 1994
Emperor Dragonfly *Anax imperator*	end May-end Aug	Last one confirmed on St Mary's 2001 and possibly 2006
Golden-ringed Dragonfly *Cordulegaster boltonii*	end May-mid Sept	Found on Tresco 1996
Common Green Darner *Anax junius*	late Sept-early Oct	N. American vagrant, St Agnes, also Tresco and St Mary's 1999
Migrant Hawker *Aeshna mixta*	late July-end Oct	Seen on all main islands since 1992
Red-veined Darter *Sympetrum fonscolombi*	early June-late Oct	Found Tresco and St Agnes
Ruddy Darter *Sympetrum sanguineum*	early June-early Sept	Found St Martin's 2003
Southern Hawker *Aeshna cyanea*	early July-mid Oct	Found St Mary's 1992 & again in 1996 when also seen Tresco
Yellow-winged Darter *Sympetrum flaveolum*	late June-mid Sept	European vagrant, St Mary's 1995
Lesser Emperor *Anax parthenope*	June-Oct	First seen St Mary's 2005 and again 2006

Common Hawker Dragonfly mating

Beetles

Beetles are big in the insect world, and on the British mainland some 4,000 different species have been recorded so far. Yet in Scilly only 380 different ones have been found. The Rose Chafer, Oil Beetle and Minotaur Beetle are the most interesting and obvious.

Rose Chafer
Only the large, brilliant green Rose Chafer is especially widespread, however, being found on seven of the islands. It is harmless, and like many beetles its larvae consume plant roots while the adults have an appetite for petals. Seen from midsummer throughout the warmest months basking in the sun, they can most frequently be found on Thrift or Wild Carrot. However, there is another much rarer form. A black variety of Rose Chafer can occasionally be seen. Apart from the colour they appear identical, but the dark relation is only found elsewhere in the Channel Islands and on Corsica in the Mediterranean.

Oil Beetle
More formidable-looking but equally harmless as far as people are concerned, the Oil Beetle is very distinctive – big, black and slow-crawling. The name comes from its habit of discharging an unpleasant fluid when repelling predators. Its life-cycle is intriguing. In spring the female beetle lays several hundred eggs, which hatch into extremely active minute yellow creatures with long legs and bristles. These swarm over the grass and flowers, climbing upwards at every opportunity, because their lives depend on the chance of meeting a bee. To survive, the offspring must hitch a lift back to the bee's nest where they raid one of the bee nursery cells and gorge themselves on the eggs. Afterwards they undergo a complex change and then take over the food store intended for the larval bee.

In their frantic scramble to board a passing bee, they seem unable to sense whether they have chosen the right lift. Consequently their lives are often brought to a premature end by hitching a lift with a fly or other winged insect, so the fecundity of the Oil Beetle is offset by the inevitable death of many offspring.

Minotaur Beetle
Distinguished by three little horns on its thorax, the Minotaur Beetle can be found in sandy places, where the adults and grubs feed on rabbit dung. Such a specific diet does, however, pose a question. What did they feed on before rabbits were introduced to the islands, or did they somehow arrive later? We will probably never know the answer – it is yet another Scilly mystery.

Green and Black Rose Chafer Beetles

Grasshoppers, crickets and other insects

Only eight of the 28 known species of grasshopper and cricket in Britain are resident in the islands. The Field Grasshopper is the most common and widespread.

Grasshoppers and Crickets of Scilly

Name	Notes
Common Field Grasshopper *Chorthippus brunneus*	Widespread on all inhabited islands
Large Cone-head *Ruspolia nitidula*	First British record St Mary's 2003
Long-Winged Conehead *Conocephalus discolor*	First recorded in 1989. Wide range of habitats, coastal grassland and wasteland
Short-Winged Conehead *Conocephalus dorsalis*	First recorded in 1990 on St Agnes, now found on other islands. Coastal grassland
Great-green Bush Cricket *Tettigonia viridissima*	Probably native. Coastal cliffs and scrub, bramble, garden and hedgerow on St Mary's, Tresco and Bryher
Grey Bush-cricket *Platycleis albopunctata*	Probably native. Coastal cliff, scrub and sand dune only on Bryher
House Cricket *Acheta domesticus*	Common in the 19th century, now only on St Mary's
Speckled Bush Cricket *Leptophyes punctatissima*	Scrub, bramble and gardens on St Mary's, especially The Garrison
Desert Locust *Locusta migratoria*	Occasional visitor. Last recorded influx in 1988

Other insects

Common Ground-hopper *Tetrix undulata*	Probably introduced Tresco
Lesser Cockroach	Native
Prickly Stick Insect *Acanthoxyla geisovii*	Tresco garden and St Mary's at Old Town Church and McFarlane Downs
Smooth Stick Insect *Clitarchus hookeri*	As above
Mediterranean or Corsican Stick Insect *Bacillus rossius*	First recorded Tresco 2003

Strange Hoppers and Cave Dwellers

The famously mild climate of the islands enables some small creatures to survive despite being a long way from their original home. Others are rare on the British mainland but seem to do well here. One little creature is a New Zealand Land Hopper, which was discovered living on Tresco in 1925. Yet more remarkable is the fact that it was not only new to Scilly but also new to science and unknown in its native home. Rather shrimp-like in appearance, it lives among damp, dead leaves. It was named **Arctalitrus dorreni** in honour of the island's landlord.

Not only was this southern hemisphere migrant far from home but it was not alone. Two flatworms have also been found here. One of them, **Geoplana sanguinea** was first recorded on Tresco in 1960 but has since been discovered in other parts of Britain. It is thought they hitched a ride on imported plants but they are not welcome as both eat earthworms and can become garden pests.

Another alien living on Tresco is unknown elsewhere in Europe. In its native Australian home the tiny spider **Achaearanea veruculata** is commonly found in webs associated with garden shrubs.

Apart from stranger wildlife in the garden, the island of Tresco also claims other creatures new to Britain. Piper's Hole on the coast is a difficult and even dangerous place to visit. Here some scientists lured some cave dwellers out of the dark with a not so high-tech device – Danish Blue cheese. Attracted by the smell, some tiny white **Springtails** and a **Leaf Hopper**, *Balclutha saltuella*, known from countries as widespread as America and Australia, were both discovered to be new to the British Isles.

Smooth Stick Insect

Fish and Shellfish

MARINE LIFE OF EEL GRASS BEDS

There is a grass that grows in the sea, one of the very few flowering plants to survive there – Eel Grass. Also known as *Zostera* it only thrives in the most sheltered places, protected from the action of waves that could tear the grass from its bed. In Scilly, these very special meadows can be found in St Mary's harbour and Tresco Channel, but the biggest beds by far lie the other side of Tresco, off Old Grimsby. After a gale many leaves can be seen washed ashore along the strandlines of the islands. Easily recognisable, the long, narrow green leaves are more grass-like than seaweed fronds. The plant even has flowers, but being small and insignificant, they are not easy to see. What makes Eel Grass special, however, is the marine life that lives amongst it.

It is home to one of the most extraordinarily diverse communities of marine creatures, which are only exposed at the lowest spring tides. Some of the most interesting sea animals found here include a rare little hydroid, the **Grooved Topshell**, and the **Stalked Jellyfish**. More common are **Northern Lucina, Small Scallop, Chinaman's Hat, Netted and Sting Dog Whelks, Tower Shells, Sand Lance, Peacock Worm, Myxicola Fan Worm, Snakelock Anemone, Sponge, Hermit Crab, Sea Potato, Shrimp, Prawn, Sea Squirt, Pipefish, Wrasse, Goby** and **Spined Stickleback**.

Another extraordinary creature is sometimes discovered clinging to the Eel Grass. The **Sea Horse** is an unusual and enchanting creature. Found only in a few very sheltered locations around the south-west coast, they are rarely seen in the wild and we know little about their lives. Living in deep water throughout the coldest months they only appear in the shallows to breed. Male Sea Horses look after their mate's eggs in a special pouch. The tiny young are liberated soon after hatching and must fend for themselves. Hiding amongst the Eel Grass and holding on with their tails, they feed on plankton. Perhaps, with their superbly camouflaged colours, they are not so much rare as just easily overlooked.

SHORE LIFE

Montague's Blenny is rarely found along the mainland south coast of England, yet is the most common fish in rock pools in Scilly. More extraordinary is the presence of creatures that normally live in much deeper water. The **Rose Feather Star** uses its delicate arms not only for catching plankton but also for swimming. Its stroke is a slow undulating motion, little changed over millions of years from a time when creatures just like it paddled through prehistoric seas. Normally living in deep water, here it can be found between the tides. Even humble **Hermit Crabs** merit a second glance. In 1962, a species new to Britain was discovered hiding in its shell, waving its brilliant violet antennae. Previously it was only known around Mediterranean shores and up the Atlantic coast as far as Brittany.

Rocky shores are usually divided into zones: the upper, middle and lower shore and the *Laminaria* zone, the deep water below the lower shore. High tide brings out the **Black Periwinkle** to graze the lichen on the *upper rocky shore*. Tiny scavengers roam

Snakelock Anemone

these finely nibbled lichen lawns. **Sea Slater** look like large woodlice, and along with **Marine Bristle Tails**, feed mainly at night. But life here in rough weather can be tough. The **Acorn Barnacle** probably has the best protection of all. Cemented to the rock, it grows where no other life can survive. At high water it snatches at passing plankton, using hairy legs as filters. At low tide it battens down the hatches.

Different periwinkles live at different levels on the shore. **Rough Periwinkle** can wedge themselves into cracks and crevices if waves threaten to dislodge them. Their rough shells appear to give them a better grip than smooth sided ones. Even if they do get washed down the shore, like all periwinkles they seem to know their place and simply migrate back again.

The most obvious inhabitants of the *middle shore* are the crabs. What a whopper! The delight of finding a large crab on the shore is one of the delights of a seaside holiday. The **Edible Crab** is migratory, living and spawning offshore. A female crab can carry over 800,000 eggs underneath her body. Hatching releases the tiny larvae to take their chance in the current. They become part of the plankton, the free floating soup of miniature life that forms the base of a food chain in the sea. The larvae settle as young crabs on the shore and as they mature they move into deeper water. Keeping young an old apart is one way to reduce competition. **Shore Crabs** cope better with the vagaries of living between the tides, remaining even as large adults, low down on the shore.

Two types of periwinkle are usually common on the middle shore around the British coast. The **Flat Periwinkle** lives and feeds on the **Bladderwrack**, while the **Edible Periwinkle** grazes the rock surface. Although generally the most widespread of its kind found on all types of rocky shore, the edible variety is rare in Scilly.

Snakelock Anemone is confined to pools and Eel Grass beds at low tide, but

Montague's Blenny

Beadlet Anemone can survive out of water by withdrawing its tentacles. It can often be found above pools clinging to overhangs and shady rock walls.

The shape and strength of a Limpet shell might lead one to suppose that it is a creature evolved to survive big waves and big bird beaks, and you would be right. It is not restricted to any one zone on the shore. Its large muscular foot clamps down hard, creating a vacuum to prevent it from drying out or being easily dislodged. Limpets also vary in shape. Flatter ones live in the most sheltered places, tall domed ones wherever there are more waves, usually higher up the shore.

The **Common Mussel** – which is not so common in Scilly – attaches itself to the rocks by threads, with large numbers often huddled together. It is a filter feeder, drawing water between its shells through a siphon. Despite its thick shell, it is preyed upon by many creatures. **Starfish**, **Dog Whelk** and **Oystercatcher** will all feed on them. Given half a chance, if a shell is gaping, even crabs will have a go.

On the *Lower Shore*, **Bread Crumb Sponge** tends to grow encrusting the rocks in the humid shelter of brown seaweeds. Other animals actually live on the fronds of these algae. Several different types of hydroids, tiny colonial creatures, grow on stalks attached to the seaweed. They feed like miniature anemones, catching particles of food on tentacles.

Topshells superficially resemble periwinkles but can easily be distinguished by a little depression in the centre of the underside of their shells. Their tops are also often worn, revealing a glistening underlayer of mother-of-pearl. **Purple, Grey and Thick Topshells** can all be found, but the biggest and most beautiful is the Painted Topshell.

Sea Slug, Scale Worm and **Tube Worm** can also all be found on the lower shore. They are all vulnerable to drying out and can only survive out of water for a short time. Even the most common fish of the lower shore, the **Blenny**, can tolerate being out of water as long as it remains moist.

A small mollusc, the **Blue-rayed Limpet** actually lives on the kelp which gives the *Laminaria* zone its name. Between, small fish shelter: **Rocklings** and **Shanny** are common, and **Gold-sinny Wrasse, Butterfish, Cornish Lumpsucker, Long-spined Sea Scorpion** and **Lesser Sand Eel** can all be caught in a small net. Even the young of more open-water fish take shelter in this zone – **Pollack, Mullet** and **Whiting**.

The constant movement of sand on *sandy shores* means that plants cannot get a grip, and the few creatures that live here survive by digging. The burrowing **Sea Urchin** and **Sand Eel** can both be found in fine sand here. The **Purple Heart Urchin** is another Scilly speciality that can be found in the intertidal areas around the islands. But danger can lurk in these undersea deserts. The notorious **Weever Fish** bury themselves in the sand, leaving just the tip of their dorsal fin exposed. If the fish is disturbed, the fin is raised and carries a painful poison. Injected into the bare foot of an unwary bather the result can be excruciating. Thankfully they are not common in Scilly.

Wind is used as a form of propulsion by some warm-sea creatures. The **Violet Sea Snail** floats beneath a raft of bubbles in search of its favourite prey – vast swarms of **By-the-wind Sailors**. At first glance the latter appear to be small jellyfish, but they actually belong to another group of complex colonial marine animals. Closely related, the infamous **Portuguese Man-of-war** also uses the wind as a means of propulsion. They too have a float, albeit bigger and gas-filled, which catches the breeze. Thankfully while By-the-wind Sailors are often found on the shores of Scilly their bigger, more dangerous relative is rare in British waters.

WRECK LIFE

The Isles of Scilly probably have more wrecks than any equivalent area around the coast of Britain. A history of shipping lies rotting on the seabed around the islands in various states of decay. While most wooden hulls have long since gone, bronze cannons, iron ribs, engine blocks and boilers last much longer. They offer a rich hunting ground for scuba divers but the real sunken treasure here is the wealth of marine life. Pollack now patrol many old vessels. **Jewel Anemone** and **Cuckoo Wrasse** rival each other as the most colourful creatures, while clusters of **Dead-man's Fingers**, sponges and fan corals colonise the deeper wrecks. The soft corals also add an exotic look, with nationally rare **Sunset Coral, Cup Coral,** and **Gold and Scarlet Star Coral.**

SHARKS AND OTHER FISH

Some 32 different sharks and around 30 species of skate and ray have been recorded in British waters, several of these from the deep water surrounding the Isles of Scilly. Sharks seldom venture closer than ten miles off the mainland coast so the islands are a great place to keep an eye open for some of these increasingly rare predators. Mako and Porbeagle are reported most years but others are less frequent.

The most commonly encountered, however, is the biggest of them all. The **Basking Shark** is a harmless giant. It feeds on plankton around the south-west coast during the warmest months of the year. They are fair weather summer visitors, often seen alone but sometimes in numbers of up to 30 or more in a loose group. Cruising close to the surface where plankton is concentrated by tidal streams, they can easily be followed at a safe distance by boat. Swimming along, their lazy motion is deceptive. In reality they are filtering up to 1,000 tonnes of water an hour, sieving vast quantities of plankton from the sea. The efficiency of their feeding technique can be judged by the fact that they can reach up to 12 metres long and weigh over four tonnes. In size they are second only to the tropical Whale Shark – the largest fish in the sea. Although Basking Sharks are completely harmless to humans, like all such creatures they have a surprising turn of speed but no brakes. Keeping your distance in a boat will help to avoid a collision.

Another large creature from warmer waters encountered off Scilly is the **Sunfish.** Situated at the end of the Gulf Stream the islands seem to get more than their fair share of exotic flotsam and jetsam. The only record of a **Swordfish** in Britain comes from Scilly, where one was found on a beach!

Violet Sea Snail and By-the-wind Sailor

Sharks and some Near Relatives found around Isles of Scilly

Angel Shark *Squatina squatina*	Sometimes known as monkfish, formerly abundant, now rare
Basking Shark *Cetorhinus maximus*	Commonly encountered plankton-feeder close to surface during summer months
Blue Shark *Prionace glauca*	Wide ranging, frequent offshore
Blunt-nosed Six-gill Shark *Hexanchus griseus*	Deep water species once thought very rare, but small ones suggest a possible breeding ground off SW mainland coast
Mako Shark *Isurus oxyrhynchus*	Warm water shark, scarce, only in SW waters
Porbeagle Shark *Lamna nasus*	Sometimes known as the mackerel shark, hunt in small groups, will frequent reefs and wrecks
Thresher Shark *Alopias vulpinus*	Has an elongated tail as long as body
Lesser Spotted Dogfish *Scyliorhinus caniculus*	Bottom-dwelling. feeding on crabs and shrimps
Nurse Hound *Scyliorhinus stellaris*	Frequents rough or rocky bottom and areas where there is good weed cover
Smooth Hound *Mustelus mustelus*	Most common in coastal waters
Spur Dog *Squalus acanthias*	Mostly mid-water and bottom schooling
Starry Smooth Hound *Mustelus asterias*	Most common of the two UK smooth hounds
Tope *Galeorhinus galeus*	Frequent, UK record over 80lbs

Edible Crab

Exotic Marine Vagrants, Flotsam and Jetsam

A variety of exotic plants and animals has been seen around Scilly or discovered washed up on the shores.

Mediterranean-Atlantic
Maned Seahorse *Hippocampus ramulosus*
Marbled Electric Ray *Torpedo marmorata*
Mediterranean Purple Sea-urchin *phaerechinus granularis*
Neptune Grass (Sea-balls of) *Posidonia oceanica*
Pink Tunny *Luva luva*
Puffer fish *Lagocephalus lagocephalus*
Sunfish *Mola mola*
Swordfish *Xiphias gladius*
Trigger fish *Balistes carolinensis*

From Caribbean and Gulf of Mexico
Blue Marlin *Makira nigricans*
Horse-eye Bean *Macuna urens*
Leatherback Turtle *Dermochelys coriacea*
Loggerhead Turtle *Caretta caretta*
Lucky Bean (Sea Heart) *Entada gigas*
Sail Fish *Istiophorus platypterus*

Southern Distribution
By-the-wind Sailor *Velella velella*
Grey Shark *Hexanchus griseus*
Porbeagle Shark *Lamna nasmo*
Violet Sea-snail *Janthina jathina*
Wreckfish *Polyprion americans*

FISH & SHELLFISH

Further Information

TRAVEL

Isles of Scilly Travel Centre
Quay Street, Penzance, Cornwall TR18 4BZ
0845 710 5555 www.ios-travel.co.uk

Isles of Scilly Steamship Company
Steamship House, Quay Street, Penzance, Cornwall TR18 4BD
Tel: (01736) 362009/362124 sales@islesofscilly-travel.co.uk

British Airways Helicopters
From Penzance to St Mary's and Tresco
01736 363871 www.islesofscillyhelicopter.com

The Scillonian Passenger Ferry service
from Penzance to Scilly
0845 710 5555

Isles of Scilly Skybus
Direct flights from Bristol, Exeter, Newquay and Land's End
0845 710 5555

ISLES OF SCILLY WILDLIFE TRUST

For more information and details of membership contact:

Isle of Scilly Wildlife Trust
Carn Thomas, Strand, St Mary's, Isles of Scilly 01720 422153
www.ios-wildlifetrust.org enquiries@ios-wildlifetrust.org.uk

ISLES OF SCILLY MUSEUM

The Isles of Scilly Museum, Church Street, St Mary's. Tel: 01720 422337

READING

Books and maps are easily available on the islands but few shops stock them on the mainland. The Isles of Scilly Wildlife Trust has a shop on St Mary's Quay with a good selection of booklets. My recommended wildlife identification guides: Frank Gibson's superb photographic books.

Index

Page numbers in *italic* refer to illustrations.

Abbey Gardens, Tresco *50*, 51-6, 111, 185
Abbey Pool, Tresco 58
accomodation 39
Acorn Barnacle 210
Adder's-tongue ferns 69, 70, 76, 128, 143
Agapanthus 58, 112, 130, 131, *134*, 138
Agimore Pool, St Mary's 45
agriculture
  early develpment 26-8
  farmland habitat 107-8
  flower farming 31-2, 39
Alder 41
algae 127-8
  see also Kelp; seaweed
Amorel's Cottage, Samson 81
amphibians 183
anemones 19, 122, *208*, 210-11, 213
Annet 85-91, 137, 149
  quick guide 37
ants 63, 185-7
Apple of Peru 131
Appletree Bay, Tresco 57
archeological sites 39
  collection of artefacts at museuem, St Mary's 101
  collection of artefacts at Valhalla 56
  prehistoric stone wall 73
  see also settlements, early; standing stones; tombs
Arctalitrus dorreni (a land hopper) 206
Arthur, King 21
Association, HMS 104
Auk 152
  see also Guillemot; Puffin; Razorbill
Autumn Lady's-tresses 69, 70, 76, 131

Babington's Leek 70, 131, 138, *142*, 142
  on Tresco 57, 58

Balm-leaved Figwort 94, 101, 131, 138, 142, *143*
  in cover of bracken 81, 93
  rare moth attracted by 199
  on the shore 70
  on Tresco 58
Bant's Carn, St Mary's 39
Bar Point, St Mary's 46
Bar, The, St Agnes and Gugh 67
Barn Owl 14
Basking Shark 213
Bass 28
Bathinghouse Porth, Tresco 56
bats 14, 182
beachcombing 121, 125
beaches 36, 121-2, 124-5
  on Annet *88*
  Pelistry Bay 46
  shell beaches 124
  on St Agnes 70
  on St Martin's 61, 63-4
  on Tresco 58, *125*
  see also dunes; shore life
Beadlet Anemone 211
Beaked Tasselweed 76
Bear's Breech 131, *145*
Bee-eaters 156
bees 111, 185, 188-93
  Oil Beetle's dependence on 205
  Scilly Bee *34*, 189, *190-1*
beetles *47*, 111, 204-5
Bell Heather 56, 63, 64, 93, 131
  on Bryher 73, 75, 76
Bermuda Buttercup *131*, 135
bicycles 36
Big Pool and Little Pool, St Agnes 69, 70, 112
bird hides 41
bird watching 13-14, 41, 81, 118, 149, 155-7
  seasons for 36 *see also* seasons: for migrant birds
  see also breeding birds
birds
  alphabetical list of birds of Scilly 160-73

breeding 149-52 *see also* individual species of gulls and other sea birds
migrant 155-7
sea birds *see* sea birds
see also individual species
Bird's-foot Trefoil 57, 63, 64, 75, 137, *139*
Bishop Rock lighthouse 22, 104
Biting Stonecrop 82
Bittern 29
Black Knapweed 94
Black Periwinkle 209
Black Prince 30
Black Redstart 156
Black Rose Chafer Beetle *204*
Blackbird 32, 53, 82, 152
Blackcap 156
Blacksmith's Shop, Rosevear *104*, *105*
Blackthorn 141
Bladderwrack 210
Blenny 209, *210*, 211
Blockhouse, New Grimsby, Tresco 56
Blue Lily (*Agapanthus*) 58, 112, 130, 131, *134*, 138
Blue-rayed Limpet 211
Bluebell 81, 88, 131, 136
Bluethroat 156
boat trips 36, 39
Bog Pimpernel 44, 136
Bog Pondweed 44
Bog Stitchwort 44, 136
Bothams (Corn Marigold) *30*, 31, 135
Bottle-nosed Dolphin 179
Bracken 56, 63, 64, 70, 81, 93
  invasive growth 58, 76, 88, 138
Brackish Water-crowfoot 44, 58, 76
Bramble 56, 58, 63, 64, 76, 93
Bread Crumb Sponge 211
breeding birds 149-52
  see also individual species of gulls and other sea birds

Bristle Club-rush 63, 69, 70
Bronze Age 26-8, 75
  graves 39
  standing stones 61, 67
Bryher 73-9, 112, *116*
  map *74*
  quick guide 37
Buck's-horn Plantain 63, 64, 75, 76, 93
Buff-breasted Sandpiper 156
Bulbous Buttercup 135
Bulrush 44, 58
bumblebees *188*, 189, 193
  see also Scilly Bee
buses 39
Butcher's Broom 101
Buttercup *19*, 58, *131*, 135, 138
Butterfish 211
butterflies 94, 111, 194-7
By-the-wind Sailors 211, *212*

cairns 64, 73-4
Captain Pike's Weed 128
cars 36, 39
Castle Down, Tresco 56-7
castles 28, 45, 46, 56, 75, *119*
Catchfly *135*, 135-6
caterpillars 199
Cat's-ear 117, 131
Celandine 58, 88, 135
Celtic heritage 67
Chad Girt 64
Chaffinch 56
Chamomile 69
Channel Wrack 127
Chapel Down, St Martin's 61, 63
Chickweed 135
Chiffchaff 156
Chinaman's Hat 209
Chough 29
Christianity, early 29, 61, 93
Ciliate Strapwort 58
Cinnabar Moth *198*, 199
Cladophora 127
Cliff Castle, Bryher 75
cliffs 117-18
climate 18-19, 32, 127
  during and following ice ages 23, 24-5
  microclimates 39, 51, 108
Clouded Yellow 196, 197
coastal footpath 39, 45, 46
Cockle 28
Cod 28

Coldwind Pit, St Martin's 63
Colossus, HMS 81
Comma Butterfly 195, 197
Common Adder's-tongue 128
Common Bird's-foot Trefoil 63
Common Blue 94, 195, 197
Common Cat's-ear 117, 131
Common Centaury *138*
Common Dolphin 179
Common Eel 29
Common Frog *183*, 183
Common Hawker Dragonfly *202*
Common Heath Bedstraw 64
Common Mussel 211
Common Reed 41, 44, 58, 137
Common Rosefinch 156
Common Scurvy Grass 64, 97, 103, 104
Common Snipe 29
Common Stork's-bill 70
Common Tern *57*, 57, 58, 93, *153*, *173*
  present breeding sites 82, 83, 88, 152
Conger 28
conservation *see* protected species; Sites of Special Scientific Interest
Coot 41, 44, 70
Coprosma 141
Coralloid Rosette-lichen 57, 63, 128
corals 19, 122, 213
Cormorant 101, 103, 105, 152
Corn Field Poppy 135
Corn Marigold *30*, 31, 135
Corn Salad 135
Corn Spurrey 31, 135
Cornish Elm 39, 41
Cornish Lumpsucker 211
Cornwall
  Duchy of 30, 31, 51
  first island communities from 26
  old Cornish names 25
  cottage industry 64
  country code 15
Cove Vean, St Agnes 67
crabs 209, 210
Creeping Buttercup 58, 135
Creeping Sea Bindweed 137
Cretan Mallow 138

crickets 206
Cromwell's Castle, Tresco 56, *119*
Cruther's Hill, St Martin's 61
Cuckoo 82, 155, 199
Cuckoo Wrasse 213
Cup Coral 19, 213
Curled Dock 104
Curlew 70, 82

Dabberlocks 128
Daffodil *11*, 20, 32, 39, 107-8
damselflies 203
Dead-man's Finger 213
deer 26, 28, 29
Delicate Moth 199
divers (birds) 46, 156
diving 121, 122
Dog Violet 135
Dog Whelk 61, 209, 211
dogfish 214
dolphins 179
Dorrien-Smith, Robert 51
Dorrien-Smith, T. A. 31
dragonflies 202-3
Duchy of Cornwall 30, 31, 51
dunes 19, 25, 112-17
  formation of 23, 112
  as wildlife habitat 57-8, 63, 70, 76, 117, 137
Dunlin 82
Dwarf Pansy 76, 94, 131, 138, 142-3, *147*

Early Meadow-grass 69, 70, 76, 138
Earwig 103
Eastern Isles *100*, 101, 176
  quick guide 37
Edible Crab 210
Edible Periwinkle 210
Eel Grass 19, 209
eels 28, 29, 211
Elder 81, 130, 141
Elidius, St 93
Elm 39, 41, 108, *140*, 141
English Catchfly 135
English Stonecrop 63, 64, 93
Escallonia 106, 108, 141
Euonymus 108, 141
European Gorse 63, 70, 75
Eyebright 64, 131

fan corals 213
farmland 107-8

Feathered Ranunculus 199
Fennel Pondweed 58, 69
ferns, Adder's-tongue 69, 70, 76, 128, 143
field burning 32
Field Grasshopper 206
Field Pennycress 136
Field Woundwort 136
Fieldfare 156
Firecrest 156
fish 28, 209-15
fishing, Bronze Age 28
Flat Periwinkle 210
flatworms 207
flotsam 125, 213, 215
flower farming 31-2, 39
footpaths 36, 39, 41
Ford, E. B. 94
fortifications 45
Four-leaved Allseed 94, 138
Foxglove 131
freshwater wetlands 41, 44, 58, 108-11
Frog, Common 183, 183
Frosted Orache 63, 70
Fulmar 152, 154
    present breeding sites 64, 88, 97, 101, 103, 104
Fumitory 135, 146

Gadwall 41, 44, 58, 70
Gannet 45
Garden Tiger 199
gardens 111
Garrison, The, St Mary's 39, 45
Gem Moth 199
geographical setting 18-19, 22, 24, 25
geology 21-6, 45, 64, 118
German Ivy 135
Giant Echium 108, 135, 185
Giant Houseleek 131
Giant's Tomb 39
Gilthead 28
glaciers 23, 24, 94, 112
global warming 101
    following ice ages 23-5
Goby 209
Godolphin family 31
Godwit 82
Gold Coral 213
Gold-sinny Wrasse 211
Goldcrest 156
Golden Hair-lichen 70, 75
Golden Oriole 155
Golden Plover 156

golf course, St Mary's 132-3
granite 21, 25, 45, 70, 118
    imported 76
Grass Eggar caterpillar 199
grasshoppers 206
graves 39, 61, 64
    see also tombs
Grear 105
Great Bay, St Martin's 63-4
Great Black-backed Gull 64, 83, 152
    chick with eggs 150-1
    present breeding sites 73, 82, 93, 94, 97, 101, 103, 104
Great Ganilly, Eastern Isles 101
Great Northern Diver 156
Great Pool, Bryher 76
Great Pool, Tresco 58, 111
Greater Skullcap 82
Greater Tussock Sedge 41, 44, 136
Grebe 111
Green Bay, Bryher 73
Green Island 83
Green Rose Chafer Beetle 204
Green-veined White 195, 197
Greenshank 82, 156
Grey Heron 157
Grey Mullet 76
Grey Plover 70, 82
Grey Sallow 141
Grey Seal 46, 83, 175-8, 178
    breeding sites 101, 103, 105, 176
    pups 13, 34, 102, 174
Grey Topshell 211
Grey Willow 41, 44, 58
Grooved Topshell 209
Ground Ivy 81
Gugh 66, 70, 149
    see also St Agnes and Gugh
Guillemot 96, 97, 105, 152
    Puffin and 158-9
Gulf Stream 19, 23, 32, 51, 121
gulls 32, 64, 83, 83, 111, 149-52
    see also individual species
Gurnard 28
Gutweed 127
Gypsywort 44

habitats 107-25
    see also individual habitats

Hairy Bird's-foot Trefoil 63, 75
Hairy Buttercup 135
Halangy Down, St Mary's 39, 42-3
Harbour Porpoise 179
Harlequin Flower 131
Hawthorn 141
head deposits 22, 23, 24, 25
Heart Urchin 61, 211
Heath Bedstraw 63
Heath Grass 63
heather 113, 132-3, 137
    Bell Heather see Bell Heather
    waved heath see waved heath
    see also Ling
heathland 45, 64, 88, 101, 111
    Castle Down 56-7
    waved heath see waved heath
    Wingletang Down 70
Heathy Hill, Bryher 76
Hebe 108
Hedge Ragwort 141
Hedge Veronica 141
Hedgehog 130, 152, 180
hedgerows 39, 108, 141
Hell Bay, Bryher 35, 72, 75, 78-9
Hemlock Water-dropwort 44, 136
Hen Harrier 156
Hermit Crab 209
Heron 29, 156, 157
Herring Gull 64, 65, 83, 152
    nesting sites 70, 73, 82, 93, 94, 97, 101, 103
Higher Moors, St Mary's 39, 41
history of the island people 26-31
Holly Blue 195, 197
Holy Vale nature trail, St Mary's 41
Honeysuckle 63, 64, 76
Hoopoe 155
Hop Trefoil 94
hoppers 206, 207
    Sand Hopper 61, 83, 125
Horse Point, St Agnes 70
Hottentot Fig 44, 47, 92, 93, 130, 131
    bumblebee on 188
House Martin 156
House of the Head, Bryher 75

House Sparrow 56, 152
Hover Fly 185
Hugh Town, St Mary's 39
Hummingbird Hawkmoth
199, *200-1*
hydroids 211

ice ages 22-3, 24, 45
Icterine Warbler 156
imported wildlife 130
garden escapes and alien
plants 144
industry 31-2
cottage industry 64
see also tourism
Innischawe 130
see also Tresco
insects 184-207
*see also individual insect
groups and species*
Intermediate Water Starwort
76
introduced wildlife 130
garden escapes and alien
plants 144
Iron Age 28
Celtic heritage 67
Cliff Castle 75
hut circles 67
village 39
Isles of Scilly Travel Centre
36
Isles of Scilly Wildlife Trust
36, 39
Ixia 32

Jack Snipe 156
Japanese Privet 141
jetsam 213, 215
Jewel Anemone 19, 213
John Dory 29
Jointed Orange Bird's-foot
63, 70, 75, 76, 94, 101,
136-7, 138, 143

Kelp 19, 46, 124, 127-8
Kemp's Ridley Turtle 183
Kent Black Arches 70
Kestrel 75, 152
Killer Whale 179
King Charles' Castle, Tresco
56
Kingfisher 14
Kittern Hill, Gugh 67
Kittiwake 93, 152
nesting sites 64, 70, 73,
88, 94, 97, 105

Knackyboy Carn, St Martin's
61
Knotted Wrack 127

L-album Wainscot 199
land hoppers 207
Lapland Bunting 156
Lapwing 156
Late Cuckoo Pint 138
leaf hoppers 207
Least Adder's Tongue 69, 70,
128, 143
Leatherback Turtle 183
Lesser Black-backed Gull 64,
85, 149-52
nesting sites 70, 73, 82,
85, 88, 94, 97, 103,
104
Lesser Celandine 58, 88
Lesser Hawkbit 131
Lesser Marshwort 76
Lesser Quaking Grass *136-7*,
136
Lesser Sand Eel 211
Lesser Sea-spurrey 76
Lesser Spearwort 44, 76, 136
Lesser White-toothed Shrew
see Scilly Shrew
Lesser Yellow Underwing 199
lichen 56-7, 58, 111, *123*,
124, *128*, 128
Light Emerald 199
lighthouses 22, 67, 95, 104
limpets 28, 211
Ling (fish) 28
Ling (heather) 63, 76, 93,
131
as part of waved heath 56,
64, 73, 75
Little Crebawethan, Western
Rocks 105
Little Egret 124, 157
Little Pool, Bryher 76
liverworts 58, 128
Loggerhead Turtle 183
Long-finned Pilot Whale 179
Long-headed Poppy 135
Long-spined Sea Scorpion
211
Long-tailed Duck 29, 156
Lousewort 137
Lower Moors, St Mary's 39,
41
Lugworm 61
Lungwort 58, 70, 75
'Lusitanian' wildlife 24-5
Lyonesse 18

Mako Shark 213
Mallard 41, 44, 58, 70
mammals
land 180-2
marine 175-9, 182
see also individual species
Manx Shearwater 45, 70, *84*,
85, *86-7*, 149
Marigold *30*, 31, 135
Marine Bristle Tail 210
marine life *see* sealife
maritime heathland 45, 64,
88, 101, 111
Marram Grass 57, 63, 70, 76,
81, 101
Marsh Pennywort 58, 63, 76
Marsh St John's-wort 136
Martin 156
Meadow Brown 94, 196, 197
Meadow Pipit 155, 156
megaliths 26, 61, 67
Melodious Warbler 156
Men-a-vaur 93, *97-9*, 97-9
quick guide 37
Merlin 156
Merrick 58
Mesembryanthemum 93, 130
Mesolithic Period 26
Metrosideros 54-5, 185
migrant birds 155-7
seasons for 20, 111, 155-6
Milkwort 137
Mincarlo 103
mining bees 189, 192
Minotaur Beetle 205
Monarch Butterfly *195*, 196,
197
Montague's Blenny 209, *210*,
211
Monterey Pine 39, 41, 108
Moorhen 29, 41, 44, 70
moorland 39, 41
Moss Carder Bee (Scilly Bee)
34, 189, *190-1*
mosses 128
moths 69, 70, 198-201
Moths (rocky outcrops) 61
Mullet 29, 211
Musk Stork's-bill 136
Mussel 211
Mute swan 58
mystical reputation of the
Scilly Isles 18, 21
Myxicola Fan Worm 209

'Naked Ladies' (*Amaryllis
belladonna*) 135

Nance family 64
Narcissus 20, 31, 39, 107-8
nature trails 36, 39
    Holy Vale 41
Neolithic Period 26
Netted Dog Whelk 61, 209
New Grimsby, Tresco 56,
    119
New Zealand Flax 135
New Zealand Wire Plant 135
Newt, Palmate 183
Night Heron 156
Norman Conquest 29
Nornour 101
Norrad Rocks 102, 103
Northern Lucina 209
Northern Rocks see Norrad
    Rocks

Oak 101, 141
offshore habitat 122
Oil Beetle 47, 205
Old Man of Gugh 67
Old Town, St Mary's 46
Old World Webworm 199
Oleria 108, 141
Orache 97, 103, 104, 137
    Frosted 63, 70
Orange Bird's-foot see Jointed
    Orange Bird's-foot
Orchid 82
Ortolan 156
owls 14, 82, 156
Oystercatcher 58, 70, 82,
    152, 157, 211

Painted Lady 194, 196, 197
Painted Topshell 211
Pale Dew Plant 135
Palmate Newt 183
pans (permanent pools) 117
Peacock Butterfly 195, 197
Peacock Worm 209
peat 26, 41, 58
Pectoral Sandpiper 156
Pelistry Bay, St Mary's 46
Peninnis Head, St Mary's 45,
    48-9
Pentle Bay, Tresco 57
people of the islands 26-31
Pepper Dulse 127
Peregrine 95, 152, 156
Periglis, St Agnes 67, 70
periwinkles 209, 210
Pignut 63
Pigs (rocky outcrops) 61
Pink Lily 135

Pink Oxalis 136
Pipefish 209
Piper's Hole, Tresco 57, 207
piracy 31
Pittosporum 108, 141, 199
place names, Cornish and
    Tudor 25
Plaice 28
Pochard 58
Polar Bear 182
Pollack 28, 211, 213
Popplestone Bank, Bryher 76
Poppy 30, 31, 135, 136
    Yellow-horned 44, 70
Porbeagle Shark 213
porpoises 179
Port Thomas, St Mary's 38
Porter's Rustic 199
Porth Coose, St Agnes 70
Porth Hellick Bay, St Mary's
    41
Porth Hellick Down, St Mary's
    39
Porth Hellick Pool, St Mary's
    41, 44, 44
Porth Killier, St Agnes 70
Porthennor, St Mary's 46
Porthloo, St Mary's 22, 23
Portland Spurge 57, 63, 70,
    76, 138
Portuguese Man-of-War 213
Prawn 209
prehistoric tombs 18, 21, 39
    see also graves
Prickly-fruited Buttercup 19,
    138
Prickly Saltwort 138
Primrose 81, 138
protected species 14
Puffin 85, 89, 93, 101, 152
    closure of part of Tean
    during breeding season
    of 94
    and Guillemot 158-9
    nesting sites 88, 103, 104
    used for paying rent to
    Duchy of Cornwall 30
Puja 53, 53-6
Purple Heart Urchin 211
Purple Heron 156
Purple Loosestrife 136
Purple Sandpiper 70, 157
Purple Topshell 211
Pyramidal Orchid 82

Rabbit 29, 83, 130, 138, 180
Ragged Robin 44

Ragworm 61
rainfall 32
rare plants 142-7
    see also individual species
Rayed Artemis 61
Razor shells 61
Razorbill 148, 152
    nesting sites 73, 88, 97,
    101, 103, 105
Red Admiral 196, 197
Red-barbed Ant (St Martin's
    Ant) 63, 185-7, 186
Red-breasted Flycatcher 156
Red Campion 135
Red Clover 94
Red Deer 26, 28, 29
Red-eyed Vireo 156
Red Fescue 64, 76, 117, 137
Red Goosefoot 76
Red Hot Poker 56
Red-rumped Swallow 156
Red Valerian 15, 199
Redshank 70, 156, 157
Redwing 156
Reed Warbler 58, 137
reptiles 183
Richard's Pipit 156
Ringed Plover 58, 152
    nesting sites 57, 64, 70,
    73, 75, 82
    taking care of nests on
    beach 41
Risso's Dolphin 179
Robin 152
Robins (Red Campion) 135
Rock Pipit 45, 82, 152
Rock Spurrey 103, 104
Rockling 211
rocky shores 122-4
Roe Deer 28
Roman times 29
Rose-breasted Grosbeak 156
Rose Chafer Beetle 204, 205
Rose Feather Star 209
Roseate Tern 82, 152
Rosevear 104, 105
Rosy Garlic 32, 126, 135
Rough Periwinkle 210
Round Island 95
Round Rock Ledges 61
Royal Fern 41, 44, 58, 136
Rushy Bay, Bryher 76
Rye Grass 94

Saithe 28
saline lagoons 111-12
Saltmarsh Rush 44, 69, 76

Saltwort 137, 138
Samson 27, 80, 81-3, 149
Samson Hill 76
Sand Couch 63, 70
sand dunes see dunes
sand flats 61
Sand Hopper 61, 83, 125
Sand Lance 209
Sand Sedge 57, 70, 76, 117
Sand Shrimp 76
Sand Worm 61
Sanderling 70, 82, 156, 160-1
Sandpiper 82, 156
Sandwich Tern 82, 83, 152, 155
sandy shores 124-5
see also dunes
Scale Worm 211
Scallop 28, 209
Scarlet Pimpernel 136
Scarlet Star Coral 213
Scentless Mayweed 44
Scillonian, The 36, 101, 182, 195
Scilly Bee 34, 189, 190-1
Scilly Shrew 83, 180-1, 181
Scilly White 31
scrub 41
Sea Beet 76, 88, 103, 104
in maritime grassland 63, 64, 93, 101
Sea Belt 127
sea birds
breeding colonies 82, 83-8, 93, 94, 97, 101, 103, 104-5
breeding habitats 111, 118, 149-52
see also individual species
Sea Bream 28
Sea Campion 94
Sea Clubrush 44, 69
Sea Couch Grass 138
Sea Cucumber 61
Sea Duck 46
Sea Fans 122
Sea Holly 63, 76, 117, 137
Sea Horse 209
Sea Kale 44, 70, 76, 101, 110, 125
Sea Lettuce 127
sea levels 21, 22-5, 73, 101
Sea-milkwort 44, 70, 76
Sea Pearlwort 138
Sea Potato 61, 209
Sea Purslane 57

Sea Radish 70, 101
Sea Rocket 57, 63, 81-2, 137
Sea Rush 44
Sea Sandwort 44, 63
sea shells 124
see also topshells
Sea Slater 210
Sea Slug 211
sea snail 61
Sea Spurge 57, 63, 76, 117, 137
Sea Squirt 209
Sea Stork's-bill 57, 64, 76, 138
Sea Urchin 61, 211
Seal see Grey Seal
sealife 19, 215
birds see sea birds
fish and shellfish 28, 208-15
marine mammals 175-9, 182 see also individual species
plants see seaweed
wreck life 213
seasons
defined 12
for migrant birds 20, 111, 155-6
seasonal wild highlights 20, 34-5
travel tips 36
seaweed 122, 123, 124, 127-8, 130
Kelp 19, 46, 124, 127-8
in manufacturing 31, 64
seaweed zones 121
Wrack 123, 127, 129, 210
Sedge Warbler 44, 58, 137
Serrated Wrack 127, 129
settlements, early 18, 26, 39, 56, 67, 101
Halangy Down 42-3
Porthennor (St Mary's Old Town) 46
Seymour, Thomas 31
Shag 28-9, 77, 149, 152
nesting sites 73, 88, 97, 101, 103, 104
Shanny 211
sharks 213, 214
Sheep's Sorrel 135
Shelduck 82
shell beaches 124
see also topshells
shellfish 28, 209-11
shelterbelt trees 108

Shipman Head, Bryher 73
Shipman Head Down, Bryher 73-5
shipping 21-2
see also piracy; wrecking
shipwrecks 19, 56, 67, 81, 104, 213
Shore Crab 210
Shore Dock 57, 88, 93, 101, 143
shore life 61, 63-4, 70, 81-2, 121-5, 209-13
on sand dunes 57-8, 63, 70, 76
Short-eared Owl 82, 156
Shoveler 58
Shovell, Sir Cloudsley 41, 104
shrews see Scilly Shrew
Shrimp 209
shrubs 108, 141
Shuttle-shaped Dart moth 199
Sites of Special Scientific Interest 19, 39, 61
Six-spot Burnet 199
Slow Worm 183
Small Adder's-tongue 76, 128
Small Bugloss 82
Small Copper 196, 197
Small-flowered Buttercup 135
Small-flowered Catchfly 135
Small Reed 93
Small Scallop 209
Small Tortoiseshell 195, 197
Small White Butterfly 195, 197
Smaller Tree Mallow 138
Smith, Augustus 31, 51, 81
Smooth Stick Insect 184, 185, 207
smuggling 31
Snakelock Anemone 208, 209, 210
Snipe 29, 156
snorkelling 46, 121
snow 32
Soft Rush 44, 58
Soleil d'Or 32
Song Thrush 32, 35, 82, 108, 130, 152
Sorrel 63
Southern Marsh Orchid 41, 44
Sow Thistle 135

Sparrow 56, 152
Sparrowhawk 156
Speckled Wood 196, 196, 197
Sperm Whale 179
spiders 207
Spined Stickleback 209
Spiral Wrack 127
sponges 209, 211, 213
Spotted Catchfly 136
Spotted Flycatcher 155
Spotted Medick 136
Spring Squill 75
Spring Starflower 131, 135
St Agnes and Gugh 66, 67-71, 112
  map 68
  quick guide 37
St Helen's 92, 93, 149-52
  quick guide 37
St Martin's 60, 61-5
  map 62
  quick guide 37
St Martin's Ant 63, 185-7, 186
St Mary's 16-17, 38-49
  dunes 139
  golf course 132-3
  harbour 20
  head deposits 23
  Higher and Lower Moors 39, 41
  map 40
  Old Town 46
  quick guide 37
St Warna's Well, St Agnes 67
Stalked Jellyfish 209
standing stones 26, 61, 67
Star Castle, St Mary's 45
Star Sedge 44
Starfish 211
Starling 53
stick insects 184, 185, 207
Sting Dog Whelk 209
Stinking Iris 58
Stonechat 82
Stony Island 83
Stony Porth, Bryher 76
Storm Petrel 70, 73, 85-8, 103, 105, 149
Subterranean Clover 69
Suffocated Clover 57, 69
Sunfish 213
Sunset Coral 213
Swallow 156
Swan 29
Swift 156
Swordfish 213

Tamarisk 81, 108, 141, 141
Tazetta 31, 32
Teal 29, 41, 44, 58
Tean 94
  quick guide 37
Tean Blue 94, 195
terns 82, 83, 152, 153
  Common Tern see Common Tern
Theona, St 94
Thick Topshell 211
Thin Tellin 61
Thongweed 128
Three-cornered Leek 135, 190-1
Thrift 75, 81, 90-1, 103
  in maritime grassland 63, 64, 70, 76, 88, 93, 94, 101
tin mining 31
toads 183
Tol Tuppens, Gugh 67
tombs
  prehistoric 18, 21, 39
  sixth-century tombstone 29
  see also graves
Tooth Rock, Peninnis Head 45
Toothed Medick 136
topshells 28, 120, 122, 209, 211
Tormentil 63
tourism
  facilities 39
  started through flower cultivation 31
Tower Shell 209
transport 36, 39
Travel Centre, Penzance 216
travel tips 36
Tree Mallow 88, 93, 97, 103, 104, 138
trees 39, 41, 81, 101, 130, 141
  Metrosideros in Abbey Gardens 54-5, 185
  shelterbelt trees 108
Tresco 18, 51-9, 185
  Abbey Gardens see Abbey Gardens, Tresco
  channel 59, 116
  map 52
  quick guide 37
  sixth-century tombstone 29
  start of island flower cultivation 31
  strand line on beach 125

tsunamis 26, 69
Tube Worm 211
Tubular Water-dropwort 58
Tufted Duck 58
Turbot 28
Turnstone 70, 156
Turtle Dove 155
turtles 183
Tussock Sedge 111

Valerian 15, 199
Valhalla 56
Vikings 29
Violet Sea Snail 211, 212
Viper's Bugloss 70, 71

walking 14, 36, 39, 41, 45, 67
warblers 41, 44, 58, 137, 156
wasps 193
watching wildlife see wildlife watching
Water-milfoil 58
Water Mint 44, 136
Water Rail 58
waved heath 73, 75, 109
  formation of 45, 111
  thriving on thin soil 56, 63, 64, 70
Weasel's Snout 136
weather 32
  see also climate
Wee Rock, Western Rocks 105
weeds 31
Weever Fish 211
wells 67
Western Clover 69, 70, 76, 138
Western Gorse 56, 63, 64, 73, 75, 76, 131
Western Ramping-fumitory 138, 143
Western Rocks 32, 104-5, 176
  exposed shores of 22, 32, 122
  quick guide 37
wetlands, freshwater 41, 44, 58, 108-11
  Ramsar status 19
whales 179
Wheatear 45, 155
Whelk 28
Whistling Jacks (Wild Gladiolus) 32, 33

INDEX

White Island 64, 82
White Ramping-fumitory 101
White Springtail 207
White Stork 29
White Wagtail 155
Whiting 29, 211
Wigeon 58
Wild Carrot 76, 131
Wild Gladiolus 32, 33
wildlife development on the
    Scilly Isles 24-5, 26-30
Wildlife Trust 36, 39
wildlife watching
    boat trips 36, 39, 176

places to find wildlife see
    habitats
    tips 13-14, 176, 178, 189
Willow 41
Willow Beauty 199
Wingletang Down, St Agnes
    67, 70
Winter Heliotrope 135
Woodcock 83, 156
woodland 39
Woodsage 81
Wrack 123, 127, 129, 210
Wrasse 28, 209, 211, 213
wrecking 31

Wren 82, 152
Wryneck 156

Yarrow 131
Yellow-browed Warbler 156
Yellow Flag Iris 41
Yellow-horned Poppy 44, 70
Yellow Iris 44, 58, 136
Yellow Oat Grass 94
Yellow Tormentil 137
Yellow V Moth 199
Yorkshire Fog 75, 88, 137

In the same series:

Secret Nature of

Devon

256 pages, £12.95 paperback

ISBN 1 903998 50 6

Available through your local bookseller

or direct from the publishers, Green Books.